SURE
TO A
HEART

V. Plummer

When Storing Silver, Special Care Needed

Dear Heloise: I cleaned a beautiful piece of silver, wrapped it in very thin plastic wrap and stored it.

Unfortunately, months later when I removed the silver the plastic was stuck "cold" to it.

Nothing I can find will remove it. Can you help me?

SINCERELY

Many of our readers have had the same trouble. One wrote that she successfully removed the plastic by using the following method, which came from Dow Chemical company. And our thanks to them for this hint:

"In the wrapping of any metal items in thin plastic wrap, they must be completely dry and clean, and should be stored at moderate temperatures.

"To remove the deposit from the item, immerse it in a solution of boiling water, to which a few spoonfuls of a pink powdered detergent has been added, and allow to soak for several minutes.

"Immediately upon removal from the solution, rub brickly with a rough-surfaced towel. Several applications may be necessary.

"After following this procedure, one may notice a slight tarnishing of the metal. This can be eliminated by following up with a good metal polish."

And, ladies, this complaint comes from moving companies, storage houses, and housewives all the time. Be very careful when storing silver, whether plated or sterling.

THE WELL-FED BRIDEGROOM

For Mrs. Blackmore

very sincerely

Margaret Willums

The
Well-Fed
Bridegroom

by MARGARET WILLIAMS

1957

Doubleday & Company, Inc., Garden City, New York

Soup Surprises

To A $\overset{\text{F}}{*}$ W

Mushroom Sauce

Sauté fresh or canned mushrooms
in garlic butter until golden
brown. Add ½ cup of cream
simmer until heated through
Spoon over a green vegetable
for something special.

Preface

Aside from love, good food is the cornerstone of a happy household, and I feel that in the beginning of a marriage, with so many adjustments to make and so many things to do, there is very little time, and certainly not the experience (in most cases) to plan and integrate meals. Therefore, this little book.

Right at the start I must say something about economy: buy the best you can within your budget; it is better to buy top-grade hamburger than a poor steak. Money spent on good food is well spent, not only in terms of satisfying the inner man, but also why waste time on the preparation of mediocre ingredients?

Effort, however, is an essential part of any dish; without it I firmly believe that good cooking cannot be achieved. It *is* possible to sustain human life with the aid of a can opener—but not mine! In my opinion, one cannot cook fast and cook well. Love and care are ingredients as important as salt and pepper. What is your hurry, anyway? After all, feeding the master of the house is one of your major jobs. The only good fast cooking of which I am aware is that of the Chinese; that requires long and arduous preparation—not to mention the pan cleaning up afterward.

You will find that to use many of these recipes you will need a well-stocked liquor closet. A bit of wine or other spirituous beverage not only adds succulence to a dish, but satisfaction as well.

I strongly advise your reading this whole book through before launching into any one menu. I have explained things as I have gone along, and you may find yourself trying to cope with something you know nothing about if you skip around. So if you read the whole thing, it is possible that when you are faced with a problem you will remember where you saw it explained and be able to check back.

This collection of menus will, I should guess, last you a good deal longer than for just the month I have planned. You will also find that you can do a good deal of adding and subtracting, and even multiplying. For instance, from the recipes given you could put together quite a presentable buffet supper—to wit:

> **Baked Canadian Bacon**   **Cold Deviled Chicken**
> **Mixed Frozen Vegetable Salad**
> **Tray of Cheese and Crackers**
> **Hot (Frozen) Rolls**
> **Rum Cake**
> **Coffee**

If you want to be more elaborate you might add frozen **Salmon Mousse.**

I have deliberately avoided some of the more complicated techniques of the kitchen. I think you have enough to attend to without losing your disposition over a soggy cake or spattering yourself with hot grease whilst attempting to fry in deep fat. Keeping calm and cool is not the least accomplishment of a cook—or a bride!

There are literally hundreds of cook books on the market, most of them are excellent. Here are two that I think you might find especially helpful:

> **The Good Housekeeping Cook Book**   A fine all round book. Explanations of cuts of meat with charts; also cooking charts.

> **The Joy of Cooking**   Clearly explained recipes and many of them. Mrs. Rombauer covers the culinary front.

A word about monosodium glutamate: I have not put it into any of the recipes as an ingredient because I feel your own judgment should govern its use. It is truly marvelous, BUT don't overdo and don't rely upon it to cover up careless cooking. MSG is a tasteless white powder composed of tiny crystals which react on the taste buds and by so doing heighten the flavor of any dish in which it is used. It is manufactured under various trade names. By all means try it; the directions come with it.

You may wonder why I haven't used more "mixes." The answer is that I rarely use them myself and know very little about them— it is a fertile field and you can do your own investigating. I am adding a few odd recipes at the end of the book because there will be places where you will want to make changes and also because I couldn't bear to leave them out.

To remove wine stains from washable table linen, stretch stained portion over a bowl and secure with rubber band. Sprinkle salt on the stain then pour boiling water on it from a a height of two or three feet.

To remove glass stains and other marks from every type of furniture except maple. Make a solution of one tablespoon of vinegar to one cup of warm water. Use liberally on stain & wipe dry with soft cloth.

Contents

CONTENTS

Excellent

Pop In Popovers

START YOUR week on a high note with puffy, crisp popovers for Sunday breakfast or brunch. You can make them in a jiffy—just beat 'n' bake. For six popovers, sift together 1 cup sifted enriched flour and ½ teaspoon salt. Combine 2 52 beaten eggs and 1 cup milk. Stir into flour mixture and beat until smooth. Add 1 tablespoon melted shortening. Beat 3 minutes with rotary beater. Pour into well-greased custard cups, filling 64 ½ full. Bake in hot oven (425 degrees) about 35 minutes. Serve hot. 55 58

I'd like to pass on a quick and easy method of making iced tea for the Ask and Answer readers.

Iced Tea Sirup

4 heaping tablespoons loose tea

4 cups boiling water

1½ cups sugar

1. Pour the boiling water over loose tea. Cover and let steep for about 15 minutes. Strain.

2. Add 1½ cups sugar to liquid and dissolve. Store in refrigerator.

3. When ready to use, place ice cubes in glass. Add about one-third glass of sirup. Fill with water and stir.

The separate salad course is going out of style. At dinner parties in Europe you are served cheese and crackers alone between the meat course and dessert.

What we called a patty shell back in Indiana turned up as a delicious flaky nest for spaghetti with seafood sauce, as a first course at an opulent dinner in Rome last year. Now it has become a mainstay of many a chic Riviera luncheon.

Celery Fingers

1 bunch celery

¼ lb. American cheese

1¼ oz. pkg. Roquefort

3 oz. cream cheese

3 tbsp. cream

1 tsp. sugar

¼ c. crumbled potato chips

Paprika for top

Grate American cheese into mixing bowl. Crumble Roquefort. Add to American cheese with other ingredients and blend well. Cover, chill. Clean celery and cut into finger lengths. Fill each piece with cheese mixture. Dash paprika on top.

...ake Orange Biscuits

...ot orange baking powder
...cuits are delicious with tea!
...pare them simply by ar-
...ging a prepared roll of bis-
...s on a baking sheet; then
... a small lump of sugar in
...nge juice and press into the
... of each biscuit before bak-

IF YOU WANT artichoke
leaves to glisten, add a tablespoon or two of salad oil to the
water in which you cook them.

In the soup kitchen: Just mix
the following in your blender
and chill well before serving —
(1) 1 can madrilene, 1 can
cream of potato soup and 1 cup
of milk . . . (2) 1 can cream
of mushroom soup, 1 cup milk
½ teaspoon of curry powder.

**Beauty drink. For
anyone who
swears by the Ver-
mont Doctor ap-
proach, a summer
health drink. One
tablespoon apple
cider vinegar, one
of honey; soda
water and ice.**

General Information

KITCHEN WEIGHTS AND MEASURES

8 ounces	= 1 cup
3 teaspoons	= 1 tablespoon
16 tablespoons	= 1 cup
1 cup	= ½ pint
2 tablespoons	= 1 ounce
4 cups	= 1 quart
2 pints	= 1 quart

A 1-cup measure holds approximately

½ lb. butter	½ lb. sugar
5 oz. cornmeal	12 to 14 egg yolks
¼ lb. flour	8 to 10 egg whites
½ lb. lard	

KITCHEN EQUIVALENTS

1⅓ tablespoons vinegar or 1½ tablespoons lemon juice and sweet milk to make 1 cup	= 1 cup sour cream
½ teaspoon soda and ¼ teaspoon cream of tartar	= 1 teaspoon baking powder
1⅓ cups firmly packed brown sugar	= 1 cup granulated sugar
1 tablespoon cornstarch	= 2 tablespoons flour (for thickening)
1 square chocolate	= ¼ cup cocoa

Cheese Spread

Mix together 1 package
cream cheese, 1 tablespoon
orange juice, 2 teaspoons powdered sugar, and one-half cup
grated fresh apple. Use as a
spread in sandwiches or ba-
nana bread or nut bread.

Helpful Hints

TO CLEAN hardware on bu-
reau drawers, scrub it in a
solution of salt and vinegar,
and then again with soap and
water.

Sock-Darners: If the light
isn't good, and you're working
on dark hose, use a small
lighted electric bulb as a darn-
ing egg. The work will be
easily seen.

Perforations in a piece of
masonite peg-board make it
ideal for cooling pie or cake
when removed from oven. Ele-
vate board on cups to permit
air to circulate freely.

Biscuit Appetizer

Biscuit appetizers like these delicious snacks are always a welcome addition to your recipe file. Prepare rich biscuit dough and roll out to ¼-inch thickness. Wrap well-drained button mushrooms, olives, cocktail franks, Vienna sausages or cheese cubes in small squares of the dough. Sprinkle with celery, poppy or sesame seeds and bake in a hot oven (450° F.) 8 to 10 minutes.

CRANBERRY HUTNEY

ple cranberry sauce
t brown sugar
r
aisins
lmonds
r
hill
nd.

Honey Spreads Fue Fillings

Li to entertain at tea or with afternoon coffee hour? The hese delightful spreads for ty sandwiches will be just thing to win complimen

Bl enough honey with crea ese to make a spread of d consistency. Add cho aisins or nuts.

Cone-half cup butter. Ad ally one cup honey until well blended. br own or enriched r

2 half cup honey to
4 on p peanut butter.
2 Be smooth enough to spy.

cu ourth cup each of ts r s, dates and figs. Seve lespoon of candied Com esired. Add one- thoro oney and blend we

Chop one-half cup dri s. Add one-fourth cu pecans or one- fou isins. Add enough ho nd well.

S les of bread with a t of finely crystal- lize med honey.

Party Spread

Pineapple Snacktime Quickie: Make a pineapple party spread by combining 1 (3-ounce) package cream cheese, ¼ cup well drained crushed pineapple and 2 table-spoons finely chopped nuts. Spread on canned date nut roll, sliced thin.

HOUSEHOLD HINTS

After rinsing off a bunch of parsley, shake it as dry as possible and store it in a covered jar in the refrigerator.

Silver is quickly cleaned by adding 1 tablespoon salt and 1 tablespoon soda to 1 gallon water in a pan and dunking the silver in it. Dry thoroughly.

If you have trouble measuring solid fats, do thusly: suppose you want ½ cup fat, measure ½ cup water into a measuring cup and add enough solid fat until the water level reaches the 1-cup mark. It doesn't hurt fat to get it wet.

If your recipe calls for 1 egg and you want to make only half the recipe, break an egg into a cup, beat slightly, and measure out one half.

New pans, etc., should be "seasoned" according to the directions that usually come with them. If there are none, oil them well and bake them in a hot (450°) oven for 30 minutes. Scrub them well afterward.

Camphor cakes kept with your silver will help prevent tarnishing.

Grease or oil the pot in which you intend to melt chocolate. This will prevent the chocolate from sticking.

Rinse out the pan in which you scald milk with cold water so the milk won't adhere to the pan. When milk is poured out, fill pan with cold water.

The skins of peaches may be removed in the same way as the skins of tomatoes, by scalding in boiling water.

15

Chicken or bacon fat may be "clarified" by pouring an equal amount of boiling water onto the hot fat and allowing this to cool. Then the layer of fat which forms on the top can be removed easily. If you have deep-fried anything (except fish) you may clarify the used fat the same way and use it again. The fat from bacon, ham, chicken, or beef may be used for frying potatoes and seasoning vegetables, and also for browning onions.

You may use the same beater for both the whites and the yolks of eggs if you beat the whites *first* and then the yolks.

If you oversalt by mistake, a slice of raw potato added to a soup or a casserole will absorb some of the extra salt.

Use a wooden spoon for stirring, but be sure it is scrupulously clean. A wooden spoon is easier on your pots and pans than a metal one.

To loosen anything which may have spilled on the inside of your broiler, place a saucer of household ammonia in the warm broiler and leave for about 20 minutes with the door closed.

To "core" lettuce, remove the damaged outside leaves and with a sharp knife cut deeply down and around the stem part. Let cold water run through the head of lettuce and drain. This separates the leaves and makes nice "cups."

The simplest way to keep food hot is to cook in the same utensil in which you intend to serve it; that is why casseroles and heat-and ovenproof equipment are so desirable.

Keep mashed potatoes and vegetables covered over low heat. A double boiler can be used for keeping foods hot or for reheating.

Reheat rice by putting it in a colander or strainer and placing this over a pan containing boiling or simmering water (on the stove). Don't let the rice touch the water, though.

Sweet milk or cream may be soured by adding 2 tablespoons lemon juice or vinegar per cup of milk or cream.

Never pour fat down the sink; save a jar or coffee tin and half fill it with cold water. Pour the fat into either one of these and the grease will rise to the top. You may then store it in a jar or, if you don't need all the fat you have collected, the hardened fat may be disposed of into your garbage can. Bacon fat (drippings) keeps indefinitely.

Always line your garbage pail either with newspaper or especially made garbage bags.

Sinking your fingernails deep into a cake of soap will protect them from the vicissitudes of household work.

Dip a damp cloth into some tobacco ashes and rub lightly over any surfaces stained by alcohol.

Rub a piece of raw, peeled potato dipped in some cleansing powder over discolored knives, forks, or spoons to remove the stains.

Keep eggs in a covered bowl or container in the refrigerator.

Cooking soda sprinkled liberally behind the books on shelves will prevent them from mildewing.

To unmold anything molded—including aspic—first, run a sharp knife around the outside edges of the mold. Wring out a dishcloth in very hot water and surround your mold with the cloth; you probably will have to repeat the operation 3 or 4 times. Take whatever serving dish you will be using, place it on top of the mold, and turn the whole thing upside down, so that the dish is on the bottom. If the aspic doesn't slide out, repeat the hot-towel application. You may even have to give the mold a few severe raps on the counter top in order to loosen the aspic.

How to Cook Shrimp

You may buy either fresh, frozen, or canned shrimp. Fresh shrimp are purchased either with or without the heads. There seem to be two schools of thought in regard to the removal of the black (intestinal) vein which runs down the back of the shrimp. Some people advocate its removal, others shrug their shoulders and disregard it completely. You will have to make up your own mind. If you remove the vein, use a sharp knife; it's a tedious job, and a little easier to do if you cook the shrimp first. The vein is harmless; it is mostly a question of aesthetics.

Excellent shrimp or crab "boils" may be bought ready-made. If you do not wish to use an already-prepared boil, cook the shrimp as follows:

In a good-sized pot, put 4 cups water, ½ lemon, sliced, 1 small toe garlic or ½ large one, 1 bay leaf, 1 large stalk celery with the leaves left on and the stalk broken into a couple of pieces, 1 table-spoon salt, a dash of cayenne and 3-4 peppercorns.

Simmer all this in the *covered* pot for 15 minutes and then add the washed and drained shrimp. Let the shrimp simmer for about 15 minutes, or until they are a bright pink.

Let the shrimp cool in the court bouillon, then drain and re-move the heads, shells, and tails. If you are going to keep them until tomorrow, do not unshell them; store them in the refrigerator as they are.

Keep 1 paring knife to be used for citrus fruit alone. The acid of the fruit will dull knife blades.

SOME COOKING TERMS DEFINED

BAKE To cook in a heated oven. Meats cooked in the oven are "roasts," except ham, which is "baked." (I've never understood why.)

BASTE To spoon liquid over the surface of roasting or baking meat; either the juices from the pan or additional liquid.

BEAT To make any mixture smooth by blending in a rapid circular motion with a beater; spoon, rotary, or electric beater.

BLEND To mix ingredients thoroughly until they are combined.

BOIL Water boils at 212° at sea level. The liquid rises rapidly and breaks into bubbles on the surface.

BOUQUET GARNI The classic bouquet garni is composed of a sprig or two of parsley, one bay leaf, and a little thyme.

BROIL To cook under the broiler or in your stove, or on a charcoal grill. The heat is directly over or under the food.

BRUSH To apply by means of a small brush or piece of waxed paper a thin film of cream, beaten egg, egg white, or fat.

CUBE To cut into cubes slightly larger than dice.

DICE To cut into small cubes.

DRAIN To allow superfluous liquid to run off of or out of whatever the object may be.

DRIPPINGS Whatever liquid remains in a pan after meat or fowl has been cooked. The grease poured from frying bacon, for instance, is "bacon drippings."

EGGS Slightly Beaten   Yolks and whites just blended.
      Well Beaten   Yolks and whites light and foamy.
      Stiffly Beaten Whites They stand in peaks, not dry but glossy.
      Well-Beaten Yolks   They become thick and lemon-colored.

FAT Vegetable or animal fat, lard or oil, also peanut oil.

19

FOLD IN   To pile a lighter ingredient on a heavier one and then blending gently with an over-and-over motion, bringing some of the bottom mixture up to the top and continuing until the ingredients are combined.

FRY   To cook in hot fat. That means oil too.

GARNISH   To decorate the completed dish, usually after it has been transferred to a serving dish or platter.

GIBLETS   The insides of fowl—heart, liver, gizzard.

GRATE   To rub whatever is to be grated up and down on a "grater"—a prickly-looking object. For lemons and oranges use medium-sized grater. Do not grate through to the white part of the rind of the fruit.

GREASE   To spread a thin film of oil or fat evenly over the bottom and sides of any utensil indicated in the recipe.

KIRSCH   A liqueur made out of the European wild cherry.

MINCE   To reduce to very fine particles by cutting or chopping or snipping with shears. Finer than chopping.

MIX   To blend by beating or stirring.

ONION JUICE PULP   Scrape the center of a cut, peeled onion with a spoon. Remainder of onion may be wrapped in waxed paper and kept in the refrigerator.

SALAD OIL   Also cooking oil and olive oil (not peanut oil).

SALT   Approximately: 1 teaspoon per quart of soup or sauce
                          1 teaspoon per pound of meat
                          ½ teaspoon per quart of water

SALT AND PEPPER MIXED   1½ teaspoons salt and ¼ teaspoon pepper.

SAUTÉ   To cook lightly in just a little fat.

SCALDED MILK   Milk is "scalded" when little beads appear around the edge of the milk. Use a small saucepan or a double boiler.

SEAR   To brown the surface of meat very quickly over high heat in a skillet, casserole, pan, or in a broiler. Also known as "to seize."

20

SEASONED FLOUR   Mix ½ cup flour with 1½ teaspoons salt and ¼ teaspoon pepper.

SHORTENING   Any vegetable or animal fat that can be used in baking—usually solid.

SHRED   To cut with a knife, shears, or a shredder into very thin slices or strips. Larger strips are called "julienne."

SIMMER   To cook in liquid that is just below boiling. The bubbles break the surface slowly and only occasionally.

STIR   To blend ingredients by using a spoon in a slow circular motion. A slow beating.

TOAST   To brown in a broiler, toaster, or in the oven.

WHIP   To beat rapidly, with an electric or rotary beater or wire whisk, so that air is incorporated into a mixture.

Other definitions are incorporated in the recipes.

TABLES

OVEN TEMPERATURES

Slow oven	275°–325°
Moderate oven	325°–375°
Moderately hot	375°–425°
Hot oven	425°–475°
Very hot	475°–500°

SIZES OF CANS

8 ounce	can contains 8 ounces or 1 cup
No. 1	can contains 11 ounces or 1⅓ cups
No. 1½	can contains 16 ounces or 2 cups
No. 2	can contains 20 ounces or 2½ cups
No. 2½	can contains 28 ounces or 3½ cups

Cans come larger than No. 2½, but you probably will not use a bigger size.

WEIGHTS AND MEASURES

Pinch	less than 1/8 teaspoon
Dash	the same as a pinch
1 teaspoon	⅓ tablespoon
3 teaspoons (solid)	1 tablespoon
2 tablespoons	1/8 cup
4 tablespoons	¼ cup
5 tablespoons plus 1 teaspoon	⅓ cup
10 tablespoons plus 2 teaspoons	⅔ cup
12 tablespoons	¾ cup
16 tablespoons	1 cup
2 cups	1 pint
4 quarts	1 gallon
16 ounces	1 pound
1 fluid ounce	2 tablespoons

16 fluid ounces   1 pint—2 cups
16 tablespoons   1 cup (solid)

EQUIVALENTS

	Quantity	Equivalent
Butter	2 cups	1 pound
Butter	1 stick	½ cup
Chocolate	1 square	1 ounce
Cheese	4 cups, grated	1 pound
Cream, whipping	2 cups, whipped	½ pint
Eggs	5 whole	1 cup
Egg whites	8	1 cup (approximately)
Egg yolks	16	1 cup (approximately)
Flour, bread, sifted	4 cups	1 pound
Flour, cake, sifted	4½ cups	1 pound
Green peas	1 cup, hulled	1 pound
Lemon	1, squeezed	2–3 tablespoons
Lemon rind	2 tablespoons, grated	1 medium-sized lemon
Macaroni	1 cup	2 cups, cooked
Meat	2 cups solid	¼ pound
Noodles	1 cup	1¼ cups, cooked
Nut meats	4 cups, chopped	1 pound
Pecans	3 cups, chopped	2½ pounds, unshelled
Potatoes	3 medium	1 pound (2⅛ cups sliced)
Rice	2⅛ cup, raw	1 pound
Sugar, brown	2¼ cups, firmly packed	1 pound
Sugar, granulated	2 cups	1 pound
Tomatoes	3 medium	1 pound

DESCRIPTIONS OF SOME KITCHEN EQUIPMENT

CHOPPING BOARD   A plain heavy board, usually about 1 inch thick, on which food to be chopped or minced is placed.

COLANDER   A bowl-shaped enamel, metal, or aluminum object pierced with many small holes, used for draining foods, cooked or uncooked.

COOKIE SHEET   A plain sheet of aluminum with a low curb around three sides. For biscuits, cookies, etc.

DOUBLE BOILER   A two-piece utensil with a lid, the top part of which fits the bottom. The bottom is filled about ⅓ full of water, which is brought to the temperature called for, and the food to be cooked is placed in the upper half and cooked, covered or uncovered. This method prevents the too rapid cooking or burning of foods, especially sauces.

DUTCH OVEN   A deep heavy iron pot with a lid. Used for long, slow cooking.

KNIFE, BREAD   A knife with a "wavy" blade—used for cutting bread only.

CARVING   A slightly broader knife, the end curving upward.

CLEAVER   A heavy, broad-bladed knife for chopping meats or vegetables.

HAM KNIFE   A long, narrow knife, tapering to the end.

PARING   A small knife with a pointed end, used for peeling.

UTILITY   A small knife used for various operations.

ROASTING PAN   A deep two-piece aluminum pan available in various sizes. The top has small adjustable vents at either end to allow steam to escape if you are braising with the top on.

SAUCEPAN   A deeper utensil than a skillet. Used when food is to be boiled or simmered. With or without top. Granite, porcelain, aluminum, copper, or enamel.

SKILLET   A shallow pan with a handle, used for sautéing and frying, with or without top. Iron, aluminum, porcelain, or copper.

24

SPATULA   A broad-bladed metal or rubber instrument used for scraping and turning foods or mixtures.

VEGETABLE BRUSH   A small, stiff brush kept especially for scrubbing vegetables.

BASIC KITCHEN EQUIPMENT

Baster
Beater (rotary)
Bowls, mixing (1 nest)
Brush, pastry
    small, for melted butter
    for vegetables
    for washing up
Casseroles (2)—1, 2 quart, 1, 4 quart
Chopping board
Colander
Corer, apple
Corkscrew
Cups, individual ovenproof glass
    measuring: 1-quart, 1-pint
Cutters (round) for cookies and biscuits: 1·large, 1 medium
Dishes, baking (ovenproof glass): 1 round, 1 rectangular
Double boiler (2-quart)
Fork, meat (2-pronged)
Grater, with assorted perforations
Kettle, tea
Knife, bread
    carving
    chef's or general utility (1 set, graduated)
    cleaver
    paring
Masher, potato

Mat, metal or asbestos
Mold, melon
    ring
Opener, beer can
    bottle
    can
    jar
Oven, Dutch (medium)
Pans, cake (2: 6 x 8 x 2, 10 x 5 x 3)
    muffin
    pie (metal or ovenproof glass)
    sauce: 1-pint, 2-quart
    sauce, covered: 2-quart, 4-quart
    sauce, enamel: 1-pint, 1-quart
    sauce, small (for melted butter)
Parer, vegetable
Pastry blender
Poacher, egg
Pot, deep (covered)
    coffee
Roaster, covered and with trivet
Rolling pin
Shears, kitchen
Sheet, baking
Sieves: 1 coarse, 1 fine
Sifter, flour
Skewers, 1 set
Skillets: 1 ten-inch, 1 five-inch
    iron (with cover)
Spatulas, 2, 1 rubber and 1 metal
Spoons, measuring (2 sets)
    metal (2)
    slotted metal (1)
    wooden (3, graduated)

Squeezer, lemon
    orange
Thermometer, meat
Tongs, 1 pair
Tray, utility
Turner, pancake
Whisk, wire (for beating)

Bread tin
Broom
Cheesecloth
Containers, covered, for refrigerator (1 set)
Detergents
Dishcloths (6)
Dishpan (12-quart)
Dish rack
Garbage bags
Garbage can
Hand spray
Matches
Mops: wet, dry
Pail
Pot holders
Sponge, cellulose
Steel wool
Stool, step
Table (2-tiered, rolling)
Towels, dish and glass (12)
    paper
Wastebasket
Waxed paper

BE SURE YOU KNOW WHAT YOU ARE BUYING

MEATS

Your best guide to good meat is the purple stamp of the United States Government. Always look for it. It assures you that the meat was in good condition when it was inspected. Some meat packers use the government's grading stamp—this, too, is a purple stamp and states whether the meat is U. S. Choice, U. S. Good, or whatever. In addition, the meat packers stamp their brand name on the meat. You will find that the different brand names indicate different qualities of meat.

The standard expression used to describe a good piece of beef is that "it is well marbled with fat." This means that streaks and veins of white run through the meat; this fat will imbue your steak or roast with tenderness.

Here are the major cuts of meats and a few of their uses:

Beef

BRISKET   Quite fatty. Soup and stew.

CHUCK   A fine cut for casserole and tops for pot roast.

FILET (or TENDERLOIN)   The Koh-i-noor of the steer. Solid meat, either roasted in 1 large piece or cut into individual steaks— filet mignon.

FLANK   Stew, meat loaf, hamburger.

FORESHANK   Soup or stew.

LOIN, SHORT   Porterhouse, Delmonico, T-bone, and club steaks.

LOIN END   This is the "Sir Loin" roast and also supplies sirloin steaks.

PLATE   Not a tender cut, but of good flavor. Stew.

RIB   Best for roasting either standing (with bone in) or rolled. Choicest cut from the twelfth rib end to the sixth.

RIBS, SHORT   Braised is best.

ROUND, BOTTOM   Not as tender as top round; good for pot roast, chopped meat.

ROUND, TOP Unless very choice meat, best roasted.
RUMP An inexpensive cut of beef; meat pie, hamburger, pot roast.

Lamb
Lamb is at its best from May to December.
BREAST Inexpensive. Have it boned, then stuff and roll it for roasting or braising.
LEG The leg is roasted.
LOIN May also be roasted. Loin chops are cut from this section.
RACK This produces the delicious but expensive French rib chop and the ditto crown roast.
SHOULDER Chops from this cut are good and much less expensive than rib or loin chops. May be roasted. Inexpensive. Have it boned, then stuff and roll it for roasting or braising.

Pork (Fresh)
HAM Baked. (In some parts of the United States the word "baked" is synonymous with "roasted.")
LOIN Cuts from this part of the pig are loin and rib chops, crown roast, also two good loin roasts: the ham end and the center cut.
SHOULDER, PICNIC Roasted or braised.
SPARERIBS Wonderful for barbecuing or cooked in the Chinese way.

Pork (Smoked)
HAM Center slices for baking, broiling, or frying.
LOIN Canadian bacon.
SHOULDER, PICNIC May be baked or simmered.

VARIETY MEATS
In addition to what I think of as being "meat meats," there are the more or less sundry items. These are generally referred to as variety meats and are, as a rule, very toothsome.

29

BRAINS   These are almost always calves' brains. To be sautéed, preferably with **Black Butter** and a few capers.

HEARTS   The best are the lamb's or veal hearts. However, beef heart, by dint of long, slow cooking, can be made quite palatable.

KIDNEYS   Best: lamb or veal. Broil or sautée them.

LIVER
  CALF'S   The most expensive type of liver.
  BEEF
  PORK

All these livers may be broiled, sautéed, shaped into patties, or prepared en brochette (skewered).

OXTAILS   Don't be afraid of this part of the animal. Delicious and thrifty.

SWEETBREADS   Expensive. May be broiled, creamed, breaded, sautéed.

TONGUE   Either calf's, beef, lamb's, or pork. Fresh or smoked.

TRIPE   Tripe comes either in a fresh, pickled, or canned state. There are two kinds of tripe—plain and honeycomb. Stewed or sautéed, and, of course, the famous "tripe à la mode de Caen," which takes about three days to produce.

Veal

BREAST   Not as expensive as the other cuts. Meat loaf, stew, meat pie or pocket roast.

LEG   An expensive cut. For roasting. Veal round, rump, steaks are cut from the leg of the veal, and the shank will produce a good jelly.

LOIN   Also expensive. For roasts. Loin chops come from this cut.

RIB   The rib cut produces chops and rib roasts.

SHANK   The cut par excellence for soup or for jellying.

SHOULDER   Rather on the bony side, but can be roasted, stewed, or made into patties.

FISH

Fish in General

The most important thing to know about fish is that it should be in an irreproachably pristine condition; bright of eye, firm of flesh, and with no malodorous aroma. Be sure the gills show red and the scales are close to the body of the fish.

Shellfish

CLAMS Several types: cherry stone; littleneck, to be served in the shell; soft-shelled for steaming and chowders.

CRABS Two varieties: hard- and soft-shelled plus the magnificent king crab. The soft-shelled crab is a hard-shelled crab. This is a Jekyll and Hyde performance; they are really the same crab. In the spring and summer before the crab has regrown its shell, which it had discarded, it is a soft-shelled crab. Later on it becomes a hard-shelled crab. It must be very carefully cleaned, and be alive and kicking when purchased.

LOBSTERS Also more than one type—or, I should say, other crustaceans greatly resembling the lobster are called lobsters and, although very good, are not true lobsters. Lobsters must also be alive when they are bought.

OYSTERS In size, color and taste oysters vary according to their native waters. They may be bought in the shell, or in a jar or carton, minus shell. Be sure no bits of shell cling to the flesh of the oyster.

SCALLOPS There are bay scallops (small) and sea scallops, (large). The former are the more delicate and are served whole, the sea scallops should be split before cooking.

SHRIMP Remember that the heads of the shrimp are counted in the weight when you are buying. Shrimp need not be alive when bought. Prawns and shrimp are identical; the popular idea is that a prawn is larger than a shrimp.

31

Poultry

What to look for: a smooth, well-filled skin which should be somewhat damp and clammy to the touch, smooth legs and inconspicuous spurs, no pinfeathers, and a breastbone that is not bony at all but more like cartilage, and pliable. Poultry is graded from Special (AA) to Commercial (C).

Roasting chickens average 3½–5 pounds, broilers 1½–2½ pounds, fryers 2½–3½ pounds, fowls 5 pounds and over. A fowl is an elderly bird and best used for boiling or stewing. In addition to chicken, there is capon (an unsexed male bird averaging 6–9 pounds), duck (which averages 5 pounds), guinea hen, goose, and turkey; all these are known as poultry. I am not including game birds.

Vegetables

Once more: above all, fresh—or as fresh as possible. Avoid vegetables that are scarred or blemished.

ARTICHOKES Should be of a healthy green with tightly closed leaves.

ARTICHOKES, JERUSALEM Be sure they are firm and not in the least soft or squashy.

ASPARAGUS Don't buy limp asparagus, and check the heads to be sure they are firm.

BEANS, LIMA (or BUTTER) The small pods contain the youngest, tenderest beans. Be sure the pods are crisp and green.

BEANS, STRING (or SNAP) Choose thin beans of a light green color, but not verging on white.

BEETS The smaller the beet, the tenderer.

BROCCOLI The whole stalk should be of a lively green, including the head, and with fresh, unwilted leaves.

BRUSSELS SPROUTS As for broccoli, choose lively green, small, fresh sprouts.

CABBAGE   There are green, red, white, and Chinese varieties of cabbage. The vegetable should be very solid, with no leaves hanging from it.

CARROTS   The smaller, even tinier, the better. They should be of a bright orange color, with fresh feathery tops.

CAULIFLOWER   The head should be absolutely clean and unmarred, with compact flowerets.

CELERY   The all green celery is delicious, but the white is better for cooking purposes. The head—or stalk—should be well trimmed and the leaves fresh and green.

CORN   If "milk" spurts out of the ear when it is tested, by the thumbnail method, the corn should be fresh and tender.

CUCUMBERS   Large cucumbers are inclined to be full of seeds; it is better to select medium-sized ones.

EGGPLANT   Be sure the eggplant is unblemished, firm, and unwrinkled.

LEAFY VEGETABLES   Spinach, Swiss chard, mustard greens, and kale are some of the greens. The leaves should have life, and not be droopy.

MUSHROOMS   Should be moist, white, and firm.

OKRA   If the pods snap crisply, they are fresh.

ONIONS   Bermuda and Spanish onions are large, flat, and mild. Our home-grown onions are stronger, round, and have white, yellow, or red skins. See that the exterior skin is well dried and that the vegetable is not sprouting.

PARSNIPS   Small to medium are best. They should be firm and smooth.

PEAS   Alas, the French *petits pois* do not exist in this country except in a can! And these have no resemblance to the real thing. Again, the smaller the pod, the better the pea.

PEPPERS, GREEN   No wrinkles here, either, and they should be a beautiful forest green.

POTATOES, SWEET; YAMS   Sweet potatoes are a pale beige and

33

yams are red-skinned; they should be smooth and healthy-looking.

POTATOES, WHITE   Select potatoes of a uniform size. They should be firm, unwrinkled, and free from blemishes. Old (Idaho type) potatoes are better for baking; new potatoes are better for boiling.

SALAD GREENS   The heads of lettuce should be very firm and well trimmed. The chicory, dandelion, water cress, and escarole should be in as undamaged a state as possible and the leaves crisp. Avoid yellowed leaves in water cress and limp mint.

SQUASH   There are acorn, Hubbard, and summer varieties of squash. Zucchini, patty pan, and yellow crookneck squash belong to the summer squash family. I imagine you will not be popular with your grocer if you follow the time-approved method of testing this vegetable, which is to poke a fingernail into one—if it pokes easily, it is young and tender. Acorn squash should be firm and of a good, all-over green—not yellowish. The same is true of the Hubbard squash. Italian squash, also called zucchini, should not be too large—small to medium are best.

Fruit

The same rules apply to the buying of most fresh fruit as to the buying of vegetables: first of all, as fresh as possible, unblemished, clean, firm, and of a good color. Lemons, oranges, and all citrus fruits, should be firm—not hard; there is a difference. In buying melon and pineapple the nose test is the best: the fruit should have a pronounced fragrance and the blossom end should be a little soft; the leaves of the pineapple should be slightly loose. Small fruit and berries that are packed in little baskets should be shaken up a bit in order to ascertain whether or not all the fruit in the basket is of uniform quality and condition.

Alligator pears, avocados, and figs should be somewhat soft if they are completely ripe.

APPLES   Some cooking varieties are Baldwin, Winesap, McIntosh, Rome Beauty.

APRICOTS   They should be of a lovely, orange-yellow color.

BANANAS   Don't buy entirely ripe bananas—they will spoil quickly; see that they have a slightly green tip.

BERRIES   Strawberries, raspberries, blueberries, blackberries, gooseberries, loganberries, cranberries.

CHERRIES   Sweet and sour varieties.

CURRANTS   Red, white, and black.

FIGS   The Celeste fig is a delicious type.

GRAPES   Seeded and seedless; white (pale green), red, and purple.

GRAPEFRUIT   White and pink varieties; that is, the pulp of the fruit is pink. Grapefruit should be thin-skinned and heavy.

LIMES   Yellow or green.

MELONS   Cantaloupe, watermelon, honeydew, honeyball, casaba, Cranshaw, and pumpkin.

ORANGES   Naval oranges are not a squeezing type of orange, but fine for serving in halves or peeled, or to use the segments in desserts. There are "Californias" and "Floridas." The Valencia orange has a slight greenish cast, but this is normal and does not mean the fruit is unripe.

PEACHES   There are clingstone and freestone peaches. Never buy green peaches.

PERSIMMONS   Choose good, deep-colored ones.

PLUMS   May be green (greengage), purple, or red.

TANGERINES   Select good, heavy ones. Tangerines or mandarins, as they are sometimes called, may be used in desserts or compotes.

35

Packaged Foods and Staples

Always examine anything you purchase with great care. Read all the printing on the can, box, bottle, or whatever.

ASPARAGUS (canned) Asparagus may be the green or white variety.

BAKING POWDER There are three different types: tartrate, which reacts quickly when liquid is added, calcium phosphate, and combination, or double-acting (also known as S.A.S.), each of which acts progressively slower. As a general rule, a lesser amount of the combination type of baking powder is used than of the first two kinds. Follow directions on can.

BAKING SODA Baking soda is NOT the same as baking powder. It is bicarbonate of soda and is used when *soda* is called for.

BEANS AND LEGUMES (dried) There are kidney, lima, black-eyed, pea, navy, soy, and lentils. I am sure there are many more, but this is all I can think of right now.

BEETS When you buy canned beets, see if they are whole, sliced, or diced.

BUTTER Butter may be salted or unsalted—usually the former. The kind of butter known as "tub" butter is unsalted.

COFFEE Be sure you get the grind you particularly like. It may be "drip," percolator, or extra finely ground.

CORN (canned) There is "cream style," which is what it says, canned, in a sort of cream mixture. Whole kernel corn is the large, yellow grains of corn with nothing added.

CREAM Breakfast cream, or light cream, is the most widely used cream. Whipping cream is heavier than breakfast cream, having a higher fat content. Sour cream, or milk, is the result of bacterial action on milk sugar. Sour cream is usually bought in a carton.

EGGS   The regulations in various states governing the grading of eggs differ; as a general rule, eggs are labeled and graded as: fancy, A, B, or C.

Aside from personal aesthetics, there is NO difference between white and brown eggs.

FLOUR   When you buy flour, ascertain whether or not the flour is self-rising or all-purpose; the latter is more commonly used. Besides plain flour, there are bread flour, cake, potato and whole wheat, entire grain, graham, buckwheat, and rye. In addition, there are numerous "mixes."

HERBS   Herbs come dried, fresh, and powdered. There are many herbs and their uses are legion. Some, such as fresh tarragon, chervil, and chives, are not too easily available in many places. Get a small box containing little jars of the various dried herbs and do your own experimenting. The jars are usually labeled with directions for use. Don't try to keep the herbs too long—they lose their flavor. Herbs should be used more sparingly when dry than when fresh.

MILK   Milk comes in bottles, cartons, or cans. Cans may contain unsweetened evaporated milk or sweetened condensed milk. Condensed milk is the one most generally used for cooking.

Fresh milk should be pasteurized.

Homogenized milk has the cream distributed all through the milk.

Grades of milk vary according to the regulations in different communities.

Skimmed milk is low in caloric value since the fat has been removed.

Buttermilk is also fat-free and contains nicotinic acid.

MUSTARD   Mustard may be dry, i.e., powdered, or prepared. Prepared mustard has vinegar and spices added. In addition,

37

there are various makes of French, English, and German prepared mustards. Also, there are mustard seeds.

PEACHES (canned)   Also apricots and plums—purple and green-gage. Canned peaches and apricots come in slices or halves—peeled or unpeeled.

PEAS (canned)   Check to see if the peas are the size you want—whether the tiny ones or the more adult variety.

PEPPER   There are almost numberless kinds of pepper and mixtures of pepper and spices. I'm not going into all that. The most commonly used peppers are: black ground pepper, white ground pepper (hotter than the black), red pepper, cayenne, and peppercorns; the latter are the whole peppers and are what you put in your pepper mill to grind for "freshly ground" pepper. Paprika might come under this heading although it is more spicy than peppery to my way of thinking.

PINEAPPLE (canned)   Pineapple comes in slices, chunks, and shredded.

RICE   There are short- and long-grain (I prefer the latter), yellow and wild rice, also the "converted" rice and quick-cooking rice.

SALT   Salt may be of one type known as "cooking salt," or it may be "table salt," and table salt may either have iodine added or be plain. Some people are allergic to iodine, so salt containing iodine cannot be generally used. In addition, there are celery salt, garlic salt, and various other seasoned salts. Ice cream salt is used to pack with ice in freezing ice cream to hasten the freezing process. There is a special coarse salt used in a salt grinder. Salt grinders and pepper mills are very much alike, the former having a little "key" at one side, which is turned to grind the salt.

SYRUPS   Molasses—there are light and dark molasses. In Louisiana there are also "cuite," which is the heavy product of the first runoff of the cane, and cane syrup, which is mostly used on pancakes, biscuits, etc.

Corn syrup—There are three kinds of corn syrup: white, golden, and maple-flavored. Corn syrup may be substituted for sugar in times of stress and strain. I advise the use, in that case, of a recipe that has been tested for such a substitution.

Maple syrup—may be either the pure syrup or a mixture of cane and maple syrups.

SPINACH (frozen)   Spinach comes in the whole leaves or chopped.

STRING BEANS (frozen)   String beans come whole or "Frenched," that is, slivered.

SUGAR   Sugar may be made either from sugar beets or from sugar cane. There are:

Granulated—the all-purpose sugar. This is the sugar that is meant when "sugar" is called for in a recipe; another type of sugar would be definitely specified if desired.

Powdered—a fine, powdery sugar. NOT confectioners' sugar. Good in cold drinks such as iced tea, and over berries and melon.

Confectioners' or XXXX sugar—used in cake icings, etc. It has cornstarch added and is finer than powdered sugar.

Yellow sugar—has some molasses in it, a lighter sugar than:

Old-fashioned dark brown, which contains more molasses than the yellow sugar; used a great deal in cookies, and also for baking ham and beans.

Loaf sugar is the small, flat, domino-shaped sugar tablet. Cubes are about the size of medium dice and the "dots" are still smaller cubes.

VINEGARS   There are cider, white, malt, tarragon, wine, and various herb vinegars. Cider vinegar is made from fermented

39

apple juice, and white vinegar is made by fermenting diluted, distilled alcohol and is therefore stronger than the other vinegars and less suitable for salad dressings.

SOME SEEDS   Dill, celery, cumin, coriander, and anise.

SOME SPICES   Allspice may be either ground or whole. Cinnamon may be either in sticks or powdered. Nutmeg may be either the whole nut or ground.

A WORD ON WINE

A little wine added to many dishes will endow them with an incalculable amount of grace, glamour and, literally, good taste.

Please, I beg of you, don't waste your money on buying so-called cooking wines (and this includes sherry); a respectable wine will well repay you for the little extra that you may spend for it.

The only time that a really downright cheap red or white wine can be recommended is for the marinating of a particularly tough piece of meat. In this case, cover the meat with wine, add herbs or spices, and allow to marinate for many hours. Turn the meat from time to time.

One cannot lay down hard-and-fast rules as far as the uses of wines go—you will certainly find exceptions, but in general, use dry white wines for white meats and fish and dry red wines for red meats. "Dry" means the wine is not a sweet one.

Sherry and Madeira are excellent for soups, sea foods, and meats; sweet wines, liqueurs, and brandies are useful in desserts.

Not a wine, but a delightful liquor to have on hand, is a good Jamaican rum, to be used in desserts and with fruit.

If you are having wine with your dinner, you can always extract a small amount from the bottle to use in whatever dish you are preparing that calls for it. Otherwise the thriftiest bottle is the half size, but unfortunately this is not easy to find, particularly in the imported wines; however, there are several excellent California wines that are available in small bottles and these should do very nicely.

Here are some wines and their types:

ALSATIAN and MOSELLE WINES   These are dry, light wines.

AMERICAN   Aside from the California wines, we have wines from many other states: North Carolina, New York, New Jersey, and Ohio, to name a few. There are American types of Champagne, Bordeaux, Chablis, Graves, sauternes and Moselle.

BORDEAUX   Both red and white; Graves, a white Bordeaux, is somewhat less dry than Chablis. Red Bordeaux is usually called "claret." Sauternes and Barsac are sweeter white Bordeaux.

BURGUNDY   Also white or red; rich, warm, full wines. Chablis is a dry, white Burgundy.

CHAMPAGNE   May range from extra-dry to sweet (shun the latter).

CHILE   There is an extremely acceptable Chilean dry, white wine.

ITALIAN   White wines, which may range from a dark brown to light amber, and reds, some of which are nearly black.

PORT and MADEIRA   Ordinary grades of port and Madeira will do very well.

RHONE   Hermitage blanc—dry.

SHERRY   The light, delicate sherries are for drinking purposes only. Use a medium sherry for cooking.

TOURAINE   The white wines of Anjou and Vouvray are a bit sweeter than some of the foregoing.

41

AMOUNTS TO PURCHASE FOR TWO

(This list includes only the most commonly used foods.)

Vegetables

Artichokes, French	2
Jerusalem	½ pound
Asparagus, fresh	1 pound
Beets, fresh (without tops)	1 pound
Broccoli, fresh	1½ pounds
Brussels sprouts, fresh	½ pound
Cabbage	½ pound
Carrots	½ pound
Celery	1 pound or 1 head
Corn	1 ear per person
Eggplant	1 small
Lima beans, fresh unshelled	1–1½ pounds
Mushrooms	½ pound
Onions	1 pound
Peas, fresh unshelled	1–1½ pounds
Potatoes, for boiling or mashing	1 pound
sweet	¾ pound
String beans	½–¾ pound

Meats

BEEF

Chopped or ground	¾ pound
Roast, pot	2½ pounds
Sirloin	3 pounds
Steak, Club	1–1¼ pounds

Porterhouse	1½ pounds
Round	1 pound
Sirloin	1¼ pounds
Individual or minute	per person, about ½–¾ pound each

LAMB

Breast	2½–3 pounds (bone in)
Chops, loin	2
rib	2 double or 4 single
Cutlets (steaks)	1–1¼ pounds

PORK

Bacon, sliced	4 slices per person (There are about 12 slices per ½ pound)
Canadian	¼ pound per person
Chops, loin	2–3
shoulder	2–3
Frankfurters	½ pound
Ham steak or slice	1 pound
Roast loin	1½ pounds
Sausages	½ pound
Spareribs	1½ pounds

VEAL

Breast (bone in)	2 pounds
Chops, loin	1–2 per person
rib	1–2 per person
Cutlet or steak	1 pound
Calf's liver	¾ pound

43

SAUSAGE

Bologna	¼ pound
Liverwurst	¼ pound
Salami	¼ pound

Fish

Fillets	¾ pound (approximately)
Steaks	1 pound (approximately)
Whole fish	1½ pounds (approximately)

FIRST DAY'S MARKETING

This is primarily a check list; I don't suggest that you purchase everything I have listed here. Don't buy too large amounts of things that may spoil—flour, for instance.

To stock your larder for the first time will take a well-lined pocketbook; but take heart, remember that almost everything you buy will last for a long time.

You will also have to add whatever you intend to have for dinner tonight (or for the next few days) to your market list.

Baking powder
Baking soda
Chocolate: sweet, semi-sweet
Cornstarch
Cream of tartar
Flour
Mixes (This is up to you)

Canned fish
    fruits
    juices
    soups
    tomato juice
    tomato sauce
    vegetables
Frozen fruits
    juices
    vegetables

Butter
Cheese
Cream
Eggs
Milk

Beans: baked, red
Bread
Cereals
Crackers
Macaroni
Noodles
Rice
Spaghetti

Bacon
Bouillon cubes
Coffee
Flavoring, vanilla
Gelatin, unflavored
Herbs: thyme, marjoram, tarragon, bay leaves, parsley
Jams and jellies
Mayonnaise
Monosodium glutamate

Oils: vegetable, olive
Olives: stuffed, whole
Relishes, pickles, etc.
Salt
Sauces: A-1, catsup, chili, Tabasco, Worcestershire
Shortening (solid)
Spices and seasonings: allspice, chili, cinnamon (powdered
        and stick), cloves (ground and whole), curry, ginger,
        mace, mustard (dry and prepared), nutmeg (pow-
        dered), paprika, pepper (white, black), peppercorns,
        cayenne, sage, poultry seasoning

Celery
Garlic

Grapefruit
Lemons
Lettuce
Onions
Oranges
Potatoes

Soft Drinks
Wine

Cleaning powder
Detergents
Electric light bulbs
Garbage bags
Hand soap
Paper towels
Steel wool, pads or plain
Tissues: cleansing, toilet
Waxed paper

KITCHEN POLICE

General

Don't let the food in your pots cook furiously; gentle cooking will avoid tiresome cleaning up of food which may have boiled over and will prevent the burning of your utensils. Heat your skillet only a short time before you intend to use it, otherwise it will get too hot.

When food has begun to cook, lower the heat—it will continue cooking at that temperature.

When you have removed the food from the pot or pan, set the pan to soak in hot, soapy water immediately. Then later you may wash, rinse, and set to dry. If the top of your stove is still warm (I said WARM), you may put the utensil upside down on the stove top to dry quickly.

Use a metal scourer (steel wool, copper, etc.) for taking off baked-on foods, burnt-on foods, and for cleaning aluminum and iron. There are special cleaners for copper utensils. You may put a little water in a pot or pan and add some cooking soda or slices of lemon and heat this on the stove for more stubborn burns, stains, or grease.

Washing Dishes

Have water hot with soap or detergent added.

First, wash all glassware—set in dish drainer.

Second, wash all table silver—put in the drainer.

Third, scrape and wash dishes—put in the drainer.

Fourth, wash pots and pans.

If you have a hand spray you can attach to the faucet, do so; turn the water on as hot as you can and rinse the dishes in the dish rack. This will dry them quickly and eliminate a great deal of hand drying.

Dishcloths and towels:

Wash, or have them washed, regularly.

48

Clean burned pots and pans by filling with solution of 1 teaspoon baking soda in 1 quart of water. Leave solution until it cools.

Dry thoroughly before using.

They may be soaked in water to which a bleach has been added.

The Stove

Clean the top of the stove each time after you have used it. Do NOT allow spilled or burnt foods to remain on or in your stove. Wait until the stove has cooled and then clean it. When necessary, gas burners are cleaned with a plain (not the kind with soap in it) steel wool pad, and a small very stiff copper-bristle brush is helpful. The "grate" part over the burners can be taken up and scrubbed in the sink. Clean the racks in your oven with a metal cleaner.

Broiled steaks involve cleaning the broiler; pans are much easier. Let the broiler cool, then scrape off the hardened fat with a spatula and wipe off the balance of the fat with a paper towel. Wipe the broiler rack off with paper towels too. Then wash them both in hot, soapy water, using a metal cleaner if necessary. Finally, wipe out the inside of the broiling compartment to remove any grease splashings. Whew!

The Refrigerator

Cover foods which you store in your refrigerator, EXCEPT fresh meat. Remove meat from the butcher's paper, wipe it off with a damp cloth, and either wrap it LOOSELY in waxed paper or put it in the tray under the freezing unit. Uncooked berries need not be covered either.

Eggs, milk, cream, butter, soup stock, and any leftovers containing milk or cream should be stored in the coldest area of the refrigerator, the bottom section. Do not store eggs near any strong-smelling foods such as fish or cheese; eggs are porous and will absorb odors. Milk and butter also absorb odors. Keep your refrigerator clean by washing the inside (including the shelves and trays) with lukewarm water to which you have added a teaspoon of baking soda. Plain soap and water may be used to clean the outside of the box.

TO DEFROST

First, read the manufacturer's directions very carefully. If your box has an automatic defroster or is equipped with a gadget that does the defrosting, you may relax; otherwise, turn the dial to "Defrost" or detach the cord from the socket and open the refrigerator door and allow the box to defrost. Hot water in the ice trays will hurry up this process. It is not necessary to take the food out of the refrigerator unless you intend to clean it at this time. Be sure you have supplied yourself well with ice whilst the refrigerator is defrosting. The time to defrost is when the ice on the unit has got to a thickness of about ¼ inch. Never, never use an ice pick or any sharp metal instrument to hack off the ice that forms around the freezing unit.

The Freezer

Do not put the following in your freezer:

bananas, fresh celery, onions or green peppers, grapes, pears, uncooked potatoes, any salad greens, cabbage, fresh tomatoes, melon, berries, or citrus fruits.

Fish should be properly cleaned and beheaded before freezing, wrapped and sealed in special freezer paper. Unsalted butter may be frozen if wrapped in freezer paper. The butter must be made from *pasteurized* cream.

Eggs—whole, whites, or yolks—may be frozen. Break enough eggs to fill 1 cup; empty into a bowl, mix with 1 tablespoon sugar or corn syrup if you intend to use the eggs for cakes or desserts; pour in airtight freezer containers. Freeze immediately.

The whites of eggs may be frozen by pouring them into containers—nothing need be added.

To freeze egg yolks, add 2 tablespoons sugar per cup of yolks, pour mixture in containers.

Bread may be stored "as is" in the grocery store wrapper in the
freezer or refrigerator, although it may then become stale
more quickly.

Leftovers. Meats and poultry may be wrapped in waxed paper or
put into a freezer container.

Leftover liquids and vegetables—soups, gravies, etc.—
may be poured into liquid-proof containers or plastic refrigerator containers—covered.

It is best not to use waxed paper to wrap uncooked meats or
poultry. Use freezer paper, bags, or aluminum foil. Be sure to put
the date on the outside of the paper or cartons in which you are
storing foods. Nothing will last forever.

TO CLEAN AND DEFROST:

Clean the outside just as you would your refrigerator. It is time
to defrost when the ice on the inside builds up to the point where
the lid does not close properly. Take out the food from the freezer
and put it in your refrigerator. If you haven't enough room in the
refrigerator, wrap the frozen foods in several thicknesses of newspaper. Using a plastic or wooden scraper (NOT METAL), remove
the frost from the box. Wash the box out with soda and warm
water. A potful of hot water placed in the bottom of the freezer
will help loosen the ice. See that the freezer is dry before you put
the food back into it.

If for some reason or other the power fails, do not panic. Food
will remain frozen about 48 hours—depending on the local temperature. Check the contents of the freezer from time to time to
be sure all is well; if packages still have a frost on them, they are
all right; and may be refrozen.

51

FIRST AID IN THE KITCHEN

The kitchen is a very hazardous place, replete with lethal weapons and dangerous activities. The best treatment for accidents is to exercise a little common sense and caution and, by doing so, avoid having them.

Have a first-aid shelf or corner in some handy spot. In it you should have:

1 box of assorted sizes of adhesive-strip bandages
1 roll of ½-inch adhesive tape
1 dozen 1-inch compresses
1 dozen 3-inch gauze squares
1 small jar petroleum jelly (for burns)
1 bottle or box of aspirin
1 bottle of tincture of merthiolate
1 box cleansing tissues
1 small box of absorbent cotton

Hot fat is very dangerous: should it ever catch fire, quickly turn off the gas and throw handfuls of salt on the burning fat. NEVER try to put such a fire out with water. A small fire extinguisher is not out of place in the kitchen.

Wipe up any spilled grease immediately and avoid falls.

Pick up broken bits of glass by using some wet cotton or cleansing tissues.

Do not allow the handles of pots and pans on the stove to stick out where they can be bumped into.

Do not keep matches where they are likely to catch on fire.

Do not try to reach high shelves by standing on an unsteady chair—have a sturdy step stool as part of your kitchen equipment.

Never use a wet or damp kitchen towel or dishcloth in place of a pot holder.

Watch out for steam when removing the top of a pot or when pouring boiling liquid from a pot.

Some Basic Know-Hows

A FEW SAUCES

The mixture of butter and flour called a *roux* is the basis of
almost all French sauces and of many dishes besides. There are
two kinds of *roux*—white for white sauces and brown *roux* for
brown sauces. The brown *roux* is the same mixture of butter and
flour as the white *roux,* except that it is cooked for a little longer
time.

As a general rule, you take the same amount of flour as of
butter; melt the butter in a double boiler or a little saucepan (the
former is safer for a beginner) and, when the butter is bubbly and
foamy, stir in the flour and keep on stirring for a minute or two
until both ingredients are thoroughly combined and smooth. I
find that using a wooden spoon is a great help in making sauces.
If you want to make 1 cup of **Medium White Sauce,** proceed as
follows:

Melt 2 tablespoons butter over low heat and add 2 tablespoons flour and stir in well. Have ready 1 cup hot milk and
add this very slowly, stirring all the time, to the butter mixture. At first the *roux* will be rather pasty and lumpy, but
keep on adding the milk and stirring and all will be well. It
will take about 15 minutes. Now, add about ¼ teaspoon
salt, ⅛ teaspoon pepper, and a dash of grated nutmeg. Bring
the sauce to a boil in order that the starch be thoroughly
"broken down" and cooked.

The whole time of cooking should be about 25 minutes. With the addition of 1 medium onion added at the same time as the milk, this sauce becomes the French **Béchamel.**

The second basic French sauce is called **Velouté** and it is made in the following way:

Prepare a white *roux* as above, but instead of adding milk, you add instead the same amount of stock—according to the dish in which you intend to use the sauce. Omit the nutmeg. For instance, for a fish dish, use fish stock, for chicken, a chicken stock, and so on.

For a Brown Sauce

The *roux* is allowed to get a little browner and you put in a little chopped onion to brown with the butter. When it is browned, add a couple of tablespoons of meat stock. To this base, you may add wine, tomato sauce, or whatever your recipe may demand.

Sauce Mornay

To the above amount given for **Béchamel Sauce** add ½ cup grated cheese—and 1 egg yolk, slightly beaten, if you want the sauce richer. Remove from the stove and stir constantly until the cheese is melted.

White Butter Sauce

Put 1 tablespoon vinegar into a small saucepan; chop 2 shallots (the same as green onions) finely and add them to the vinegar. Let the vinegar "reduce"—that is, to cook away, not entirely, but to about half of the original amount. Then add ½ stick (4 tablespoons) butter (for two people) in small pieces and allow all this to melt whilst stirring with a wooden spoon. When the butter is melted but still white and creamy, remove sauce from the stove and serve.

Black Butter

For each person, melt 2 tablespoons butter in a saucepan. When it starts to brown, add a little vinegar—according to your taste—and a bit of snipped parsley. Drained capers may be added as well.

Tartare Sauce

Add some chopped sweet pickle, a little snipped parsley, and some capers and minced shallots to mayonnaise.

Uncooked Hollandaise (ersatz)

Beat the yolks of 2 eggs until thick and lemon-colored. Use a hand or electric beater. Add ½ teaspoon salt and a dash of white pepper. Have ready ½ cup butter, melted; add 3 tablespoons of the butter to the egg yolks, beating all the time. Then slowly beat in the remainder of the butter, alternating with a few drops of strained lemon juice (using 1 tablespoon lemon juice in all). This amount will serve four and it may be made ahead of time and kept in the refrigerator. To warm, stir until softened in a double boiler over warm—NOT HOT—water. If you don't use all of the sauce, you may keep the balance as indicated above.

BREAKFAST

Oranges

Fresh orange juice will keep its vitamin C content for 24 hours if it is stored in a covered container in your refrigerator.

You may like the frozen orange juice; it saves a lot of wear and tear.

Naval oranges may be served for breakfast. Cut one in half crosswise; use a fork to take out the seeds and kitchen shears to cut the white membrane from the meat of the orange and to separate the core from the fruit. Lift out the core and loosen membrane. Sprinkle with sugar if you like. Or you may loosen each segment separately with a sharp knife and leave the pieces in place. If you fix the oranges the night before, cover them with waxed paper and put in the refrigerator.

Grapefruit

Grapefruit juice may be treated the same as orange juice; the preparation is also the same. You may buy grapefruit sections canned.

Bananas

Don't store them in the refrigerator. Peel and slice them just before serving.

Berries

Take the berries from the box as soon as you can and remove any spoiled or damaged fruit. Keep the best berries in the refrigerator until just before serving, then wash, drain, and remove the hulls. Sprinkle with lemon juice and sugar and serve.

Figs

Keep them in the refrigerator until ready to prepare.

Peel with a sharp knife; serve whole, halved or sliced with cream.

Bacon

Put the desired number of bacon slices in a cold pan, turn the flame to medium, and cook, draining some, but not all, of the accumulated fat from time to time. Save the bacon fat. Turn the bacon once, and when it is golden brown (in about 5 minutes) remove it and drain the pieces of excess fat on a paper towel or brown paper.

Bacon may also be cooked in the oven by placing the bacon on a wire rack with a pan beneath it and baking it in a preheated 400° oven for 10 minutes. You need not drain the fat until after the bacon is cooked. Sliced Canadian bacon is cooked in a pan the same way as the above bacon, except that it should not brown, just cook through.

Sausage

Sausage comes in bulk and in links. All pork must be thoroughly cooked. Cook the required number of links, starting them in a cold skillet over low heat for 10–15 minutes or until well browned. Drain off the fat from time to time and turn frequently. For sausage cakes, which are made from bulk sausage, cook the same way as you do the link sausage.

You may also put the sausages in a baking pan in a preheated 375° oven for about 30 minutes, or until they are well cooked. Turn them once.

Ham

This may be "precooked" or canned ham. Heat a skillet and rub with a little of the fat which you have trimmed off of the slice of ham. Brown very lightly over low heat on both sides, put a cover on the pan, and continue cooking until tender. Turn the slice often.

Eggs

FRIED

You may fry eggs in the fat remaining in the pan in which you cooked bacon. See that the heat is turned low, break the eggs into a saucer, and slide gently into the hot fat. Cook about 4 minutes. Baste them, that is, spoon some of the fat over them. If you like your eggs well done, turn them over, using a broad-bladed spatula or pancake turner when the whites are partly set.

HARD-COOKED

Put the eggs in a saucepan and cover them with cold water, put the lid on the pan and bring the water to a boil. When the water boils, lower the heat and let the eggs simmer for 15 minutes. Don't forget to run cold water over hard-cooked eggs immediately, to prevent the yolks from turning dark.

POACHED

Method A. Remove the egg cups from an egg poacher and fill the poacher about one-third full of boiling water. A poacher is a skillet into which fits a circular piece of metal with 4 holes in it; shallow metal cups fit into these holes. Rub the egg cups with butter and break 1 egg into each cup. Put the cups in the poacher over the boiling water and cover. The eggs should cook approximately 3 minutes. They are done when the whites are "set" or solid-looking and there is a white film over the yolk. Loosen the eggs and slip out onto toast or fried ham.

Method B. Grease a small skillet and fill with boiling water. Add a little salt and vinegar. Break the eggs into a saucer, one by one, and slide them carefully into the water. Don't crowd the eggs. Cover the pan, lower the heat enough so that the water is hot but not boiling. Cook 3–5 minutes. Remove with a slotted turner, drain, and then transfer to toast or ham.

SCRAMBLED

Scrambled eggs may be done in two different ways: the skillet or the double-boiler method.

For two people, melt 1 tablespoon butter or margarine in a skillet over a low flame. Beat 3 eggs with a fork or with an egg beater and pour this into the pan. Add ⅛ teaspoon salt and the same amount of pepper. When the eggs begin to cook, stir them with the flat of a fork until they are thickened.

If you want to cook the eggs in a double boiler, melt the same amount of butter in the top of the boiler, beat the eggs just a little, and add to them a generous ¼ cup milk or cream, pour the whole mixture into the upper part of the double boiler (be sure you have the bottom part about one-third full of boiling water), and cook until thick. Stir from time to time.

SHIRRED

Rub several shallow ovenproof glass dishes, custard cups or ramekins with oil, butter, or margarine, and put 1 tablespoon cream in the bottom of each one. Break an egg into each cup, sprinkle the eggs with a little salt and pepper, and place the cups on a baking sheet, or in a shallow pan, and put them in a preheated 350° oven to bake for 15–20 minutes.

SOFT-COOKED
Method A. Put the eggs in a saucepan and cover with boiling water. Put the cover on the pan and allow the eggs to simmer for anywhere from 3–5 minutes, depending on how you like them.
Method B. Put the eggs in a saucepan and cover them with cold water, put the lid on the pot and bring the water to a boil. If you want your eggs soft, take them out as soon as the water boils; for more cooked eggs, turn off the heat and let the eggs remain in the hot water 3–5 minutes more.

Coffee
STRICTLY NEW ORLEANS
The white enamel or "granite" drip coffeepot used mostly in New Orleans is by far the best utensil for drip coffee. There are 5 parts to the pot, and the pots themselves come in various sizes: for 2, 4, or 6 cups of coffee. There is the bottom part of the pot into which the coffee drips, a center section which fits into the pot and into the bottom of which the ground coffee is placed; next comes a circular porcelain object with a little loop handle sticking straight up and with about 8 small holes in it. This is put over the ground coffee; another similar doodad, but with more perforations, fits into the upper part of the second story of the coffeepot. It is not essential to use these two things, but they do help to keep the grounds from filtering through into the coffee and the coffee from bubbling over.

For a really good, strong brew use 3 tablespoons coffee for each cup of water. Put the coffee in the upper compartment of the pot and pour a little furiously boiling water over it. Let the water drip through and repeat until you have the amount of coffee you require.

NEVER LET DRIP COFFEE BOIL. Keep the coffeepot in a pan of water over low heat to keep the coffee hot. Of course, there are many other ways of making coffee—boiled (ugh!), percolated, filtered, and espresso. With the exception of the boiled coffee, each method requires its special coffeepot or coffee maker.

However, the most generally used method is:

PERCOLATED COFFEE

To make 2 cups of coffee:

Pour 2 cups water into the bottom section of the percolator.

Put 4 tablespoons coffee into the upper section. Cover, and bring to a boil.

Allow the water to boil up through the coffee for at least 5 minutes; longer, if you want stronger coffee. You can probably judge by the color whether or not the coffee is of the desired strength.

COCKTAIL THINGS

Aside from the enormous number of already-made cocktail crackers, chips, snips, and snacks, here are a few that will serve to break the monotony:

Nantucket Sandwiches

These sound alarming because they are made of onions but, truly, they DO NOT create an unpleasant atmosphere. You should have the "purple" or Bermuda kind of onion; peel the onions and slice them very thin. Put them to soak overnight or for several hours in 1 cup ice water to which you have added 1 generous tablespoon salt. Drain and soak 30 minutes more in white vinegar. Drain and chill. Cut white bread into rather large rounds and spread with mayonnaise, place 1 onion slice on each round and top with another round of bread. Have the sandwiches very cold.

Sour Cream and Red Caviar

Mix sour cream with enough red caviar to make a fairly solid mixture. You may serve this either in a bowl to be spread on crackers by your company, or you may put it on toast rounds or crackers yourself. A little onion juice added to this is good. Try this spread on rounds of pumpernickel for a change.

Fresh, Raw Vegetables

These have the added attraction of being very pretty to look at as well as being non-fattening, although they do involve some preparation.

Carrot straws
Cauliflower flowerets
Cucumber fingers
Celery
Green pepper straws
Radishes
Green onions

These must all be cold. With the exception of the celery and cucumbers, which are chilled in ice water, all the vegetables are prepared and wrapped in a damp cloth before they are put in the refrigerator. Arrange them on a platter and put a small bowl in the center containing Russian dressing, mayonnaise, curry dressing, or just celery salt.

Cream Cheese and Onion

Mash one small (3-ounce) package of cream cheese with a fork and mix with a little finely minced onion and mayonnaise.

Spread this on crackers and toast for a few minutes under the broiler.

Pecan Halves

Sauté the pecan halves with a little oil or butter and sprinkle with salt. They are lovely with anything.

Cream Cheese and Chipped Beef

Chipped beef is dried beef, and usually comes in small- and large-sized glass jars. Mash and cream 1 small package cream cheese and season liberally with salt and pepper. Add 1 small onion, grated. Cut, or chop up fine, the contents of

65

1 small jar chipped beef and mix with a little cream. Combine the beef with onion and cream cheese, transfer to a small serving bowl, and chill well. If you make this in a larger quantity for a party, it is nice to pack it in a mold previously rinsed out in cold water, chill thoroughly, and unmold to serve. (See **HOUSEHOLD HINTS** for unmolding directions.)

Roquefort Cheese and Red Caviar

Cream some Roquefort or blue cheese and spread on the desired number of toasted crackers. Put ½ teaspoon red caviar on top of the cheese and serve.

PUFFY CHEESE TIDBITS
(MAKES ABOUT 2 DOZEN)

Beat the white of an egg stiff. Fold in ¼ cup mayonnaise, ½ teaspoon Worcestershire, ⅛ teaspoon onion salt and a dash of cayenne. Add ¼ cup grated Parmesan cheese. Pile in centers of round crackers. Broil 4 or 5 inches from heat for 1½ to 2 minutes, or until lightly browned.

Delicious Spread

CANNED SHRIMP are s enough to mash with a fork sandwich fillings. Add the s food to soft cheddar cheese mix in a little chili sauce fo delicious spread.

Curried French Fries with Chutney Dip

3 tablespoons salad oil
1 package (1 pound) frozen French fried potatoes
Curry powder to taste
Salt to taste

Heat oil in skillet. Add frozen potatoes. Cook, stirring frequently, until defrosted and golden brown. Drain. Sprinkle with curry powder, salt; toss. Serve hot with Chutney Dip. Yield: 2 cups.

Chutney Dip

1 cup commercial sour cream
¼ cup chutney, chopped
3 tablespoons minced onion
1 clove garlic, mashed
½ teaspoon salt
Coarsely ground pepper to taste

Combine ingredients; blend thoroughly. Chill. Yield: 1 cup dip.

Hot Dip

Here's a quick dip to use hot for shrimp or crab; or to spoon over seafood and serve as a hot cocktail. Combine an 8-ounce can tomato sauce, lemon juice, Worcestershire sauce and salt to taste. Add a teaspoon or so of instant minced onion and simmer about 5 minutes to blend and heat ingredients.

epare bacon-wrapped ripe
s in advance and slip un-
roiler as guests arrive.

ain pitted ripe olives well,
some with slivers of Ched-
cheese and other with snips
een onion or pepper.

ap in bacon strips and
n with picks. B r o i l to
bacon. Good, too, are
chy salted, or smoke flav-
toasted almonds for nib-

A TANGY SPREAD that's
delicious as an appetizer or TV
snack is easily prepared. Combine one three-ounce package
cream cheese and ½ teaspoon
salt s e a s o n i n g, 1 teaspoon
spaghetti s a u c e seasoning.
Blend thoroughly and spread on
crackers or crisp celery.

RIGINAL BOLS
RASSHOPPER

1 part
ols Green Creme de Menthe

1 part
Bols White Creme de Cacao

1 part light cream

Blend in a mixer with ice and
strain into chilled cocktail glass

Menus and Recipes

Suggestion For Cooking Minute Rice

NEW YORK— (UPI) —When cooking minute rice, put a paper towel under the lid after removing the pan from the stove and let the rice stand.

The grains will become dry and separate.

I feel reasonably sure that at least ninety-nine out of one hundred brides have lamb chops as the pièce de résistance *of their first dinner. Let us be a little different; this is divine and very easy. This menu would also do very well for a small party.*

Jellied Canned Soup
Chicken Sautéed in Sour Cream and White Wine
Frozen Peas   Converted Rice
Mixed Frozen Strawberries and Peaches

1. Buy the kind of soup in cans made especially for jelling; either Madrilene or tomato. Put the can of soup in the freezer or in the freezer part of your refrigerator. Better do this several hours ahead of time to be absolutely certain the soup will jell properly.

2. Defrost and mix together 1 box each frozen strawberries and peaches. Keep the fruit in the refrigerator. A nice dress-up touch is to mix about 1 ounce or 3 tablespoons kirsch with the fruit shortly before you are ready to serve it. Kirsch is a sweet, white liqueur distilled from the juice of the European wild cherry.

3. Buy the kind of rice that has been converted—it's a little easier to cook; follow the directions on the box and use the double-boiler method. Be sure you put the lid on the double boiler and cook the rice for 20–25 minutes. When the rice is done, tilt the lid of the pot so that the steam won't collect and make the rice soggy.

4. Cook the peas according to the directions on the back of the box. Drain off any excess liquid by pouring the peas into a strainer or a colander, and put them in a serving dish or back in the saucepan to keep hot.

Mix in a small piece of butter just before you are ready to serve the peas.

5. Buy a box of frozen chicken or the already cut-up pieces of fresh chicken. I prefer the latter because you can choose exactly the pieces you want: breasts, thighs, drumsticks, or whatever. Al-

though I believe now frozen thighs or breasts, etc., are available in many shops. Two pieces of breast for two people should be approximately enough unless you feel quite hungry. This is a rather rich dish and not particularly good as a leftover, so don't overdo it. This is how you cook the chicken:

Wipe each piece of chicken off with a damp cloth. (I don't like chicken skin, so I remove it, using kitchen shears to aid the operation.) Mix ¼ cup flour with ½ teaspoon salt and ⅛ teaspoon pepper in a paper bag, put your chicken pieces in the bag and jounce them around a bit so that the pieces are coated with the flour. This is known as dredging. The paper bag is not essential, but it does eliminate a lot of mess. Instead of using a bag, you may spread the flour on a piece of waxed paper and flop the chicken pieces around in it until they are lightly coated with the flour.

Next, put ½ stick butter (or margarine) into a skillet or an iron pot that has a lid (a skillet is the same as a frying pan) and turn the flame to medium. Butter can burn easily, so don't hasten the melting process.

When the butter is foamy, put the chicken in, breast (or meaty) side down. Do this gently so as not to splash yourself and the stove with hot fat; if you have a pair of kitchen tongs, use them. Turn the flame up a bit and let the chicken cook until it is golden, then, using the tongs, turn the pieces on the other side and repeat the operation. When they are done on both sides, put the cover on the pan or pot and let the pieces cook about 15–20 minutes, turning them once or twice. You can tell whether or not they are cooked by sticking a sharp knife or fork into the meat; if the juice that comes out is clear, the meat is done; if the juice is pink, cook the chicken a bit more.

In a small saucepan, warm ½ cup sour cream; remove the skillet with the chicken in it from the flame and pour the warmed cream over the chicken. Swizzle this around for a second and then pour in about ¼ cup or 3–4 tablespoons white wine and add 1 bay leaf. The sauce will look somewhat curdled, but relax, all is as it should be. Put the cover back on the pot and return to the fire. Lower the flame and cook about 5 minutes more. Be sure you fish out the bay leaf before serving. When I cook this for six people, I use a whole stick of butter (extravagant) and 1 cup of sour cream.

MARKET LIST: 1 can soup for jellying, 2 or 3 pieces chicken breast, 1 pint sour cream, 1 box converted rice, 1 box frozen peas, 1 box frozen strawberries, 1 box frozen peaches, 1 small bottle *dry* white wine, ¼ pound butter, 1 box bay leaves or 1 bunch ditto, 1 bottle kirsch, any desired sort of bread.

Bay leaves keep a long time and it is usually more economical to buy them by the bunch.

YOU SHOULD HAVE ON HAND: flour, salt, pepper, a paper bag or waxed paper.

If you cooked a whole cup of rice for the preceding dinner, you probably have some left over, in which case you can use it up thusly:

Rice and Ham
Cold Artichokes   Mayonnaise Dressing
Half Cantaloupe with Blueberries

1.   Cut off the stems of the artichokes close to the bottom, remove the more battered outside leaves and discard them. With kitchen shears, trim about ¾ inch from the top of the larger of the remaining leaves, cutting them off squarely. Scrub the artichokes well with a small brush called a vegetable brush, and soak them for ½ hour in water to which you have added 2 teaspoons salt per quart of water. This is done to remove any lurking wildlife. Drain the artichokes, that is, stand them upside down so that the water can run out.

Cook them in a tightly covered saucepan in about 1 inch of water for 25–60 minutes. Test for doneness by poking a fork into the bottoms.

The object of cooking any vegetable in a small amount of water is to retain the vitamins, but if you prefer to boil them in the good old-fashioned way, this is how it is done: Fill your pot about three-quarters full and add 1 tablespoon vinegar, to keep the artichokes from discoloring, and ½ teaspoon salt. Cook until tender. After the artichokes are cooked, drain them again and cool. As they will be hot, I advise the use of a colander for the draining process (a colander is a bowl-shaped object, pierced with many small holes), or you may use a large sieve. When the artichokes have cooled sufficiently, turn them upside down again so that all the water drains away.

Then carefully separate the center leaves in order to get at the "choke" or fibrous center of the artichoke. Use a spoon or a small sharp knife and run it around the choke, lift it out, and throw it away. Scrape out any remaining "hairs."

Put some mayonnaise in the center of the artichokes or serve the dressing separately.

2. Cut the melon in half and, with a silver spoon, scrape out the seeds. Chill fruit in the refrigerator.

Defrost the blueberries and drain.

Shortly before serving, fill the center of each melon half with some of the berries.

3. Buy ½-pound slice of boiled, or already cooked, tenderized ham.

Wipe it off with a damp cloth, trim off the fat, and dice.

Mix the ham and leftover rice together—the proportions aren't too important—and if there are any leftover peas or whatever, put those in too.

Moisten the mixture with some tomato juice.

Grease a casserole by pouring a little cooking oil in the bottom and rubbing it around in the casserole, using a piece of waxed paper. Fill the casserole with the ham-rice-vegetable mixture and sprinkle the top generously with grated Italian cheese. Have your oven preheated to 350° and place the casserole in it until the cheese is thoroughly browned. Quite good already-grated Italian or Parmesan cheese may be bought in little cans or jars.

MARKET LIST: ½ pound cooked ham in 1 piece, 2 artichokes, 1 cantaloupe, 1 box frozen blueberries, French bread, mayonnaise, tomato juice, grated cheese.

YOU SHOULD HAVE ON HAND: Cooking oil, vinegar, salt, pepper.

Unless you drank the rest of the white wine you used in the chicken and sour cream, you must have quite a bit left (I hope you kept it in the refrigerator), so you might use it up in this fish dish.

Crème Congolaise
Baked Fillet of Sole au Gratin
Boiled Potatoes   Asparagus Vinaigrette
Fresh Pineapple

1.   Buy canned *cream* of chicken soup, without rice, and dilute according to the directions on the can. Heat in a double boiler.

Mix a generous tablespoon of curry powder with a little of the soup separately, and then add this to the balance of the soup. Stir well and put in the refrigerator to chill. Serve in cold soup cups. If you are a curry addict, add more curry to taste and perhaps a dash of Tabasco sauce as well.

2.   Try to select potatoes of approximately the same size so that they will cook uniformly.

Scrub them well with a vegetable brush, cut out the "eyes" and any sprouts and blemishes. For whole, medium-sized potatoes, cook them in a tightly covered pot or saucepan in about 1 inch of boiling water for 35–40 minutes, shake the pot from time to time, and add a little more water if necessary.

When the potatoes are done (you can test them with a fork), drain them, let them cool a little, and then peel them.

Place them in an uncovered saucepan over low heat to dry out.

Before you serve the potatoes, pour a little melted butter or margarine over them and sprinkle them with either a little paprika or finely snipped parsley.

3.   The vinaigrette sauce looks like a great deal of trouble but it keeps well, so you will save time another day. Mix the following ingredients together and chill thoroughly:

½ cup salad oil
5 tablespoons tarragon vinegar
½ teaspoon powdered sugar
2 tablespoons minced parsley
Salt and pepper
1 tablespoon chopped pickle (sweet)
2 tablespoons finely chopped onion
8 green peppers (bottled), finely chopped, *or*
1 fresh green pepper, minced
½ pimiento, finely chopped

Buy the already-chopped pickle. The green peppers are the small variety that come bottled. As to the parsley, rinse the whole bunch well, shake it as dry as possible, and store in a covered jar in the refrigerator. In this case, take several sprigs, remove the stems, and snip them fine with kitchen shears.

I suppose we might as well face the onion situation right now. Cut off both ends of the onion and, with a sharp knife, remove the outer layer of skin (if you keep your mouth open during this operation you will reduce crying to a minimum). To produce 2 tablespoons chopped onion, you will need 2 slices, or about ¼–⅓ of a whole onion.

You should be able to chop everything that is to be chopped at one time, so assemble the ingredients on a chopping board and, with the aid of a cleaver, proceed to chop. A cleaver is a broad-bladed, businesslike-looking instrument. Grasp the handle in your right hand and hold the opposite end down with your left hand, work the handle end up and down, passing the blade rapidly over the object or objects you wish to chop or mince. Mincing means to reduce things to fine particles, and chopping is a coarser form of mincing.

Salad oil is different from cooking oil, although some oils may be used for both. I prefer pure olive oil for salad dressing.

4. Follow the directions on the back of the box to cook the frozen asparagus. Drain and chill.

When you are ready to serve, arrange the asparagus on cold salad plates or a shallow serving dish, stir the dressing until well blended, and pour a little over the asparagus, or cold cooked broccoli.

5. As a rule, sole is unavailable in this country, so you have to substitute fillet of trout or flounder; 1 medium-sized fish should be ample.

The fillet is the meaty part on the side of the fish; you may buy it fresh or frozen. If you are using fresh fish, ask your butcher or fishman to fillet and skin whatever fish you choose. Let me say right here that a friendly butcher is a pearl without price, he can save you endless time, trouble, and labor; when you find such a gem, hang on to him for dear life.

Grease a shallow glass baking dish with oil or butter, put the fillets in the dish, and sprinkle with a little salt and pepper mixed together.

Pour in ¼ cup dry white wine and ¼ cup water mixed together, then sprinkle the fish with bread crumbs and dot with butter. Already-prepared bread crumbs may be bought, but to my mind they always make a sodden mess, so make your own bread crumbs by drying out some stale white bread in the oven, placing the bread between sheets of waxed paper, and rolling it with a rolling pin. You can make more than you will actually use in the recipe and keep the balance in a covered glass jar.

To dot with butter, cut small pieces from a stick of butter and cast them hither and yon over the fish.

Bake in a preheated moderate (350°) oven for about 25 minutes, or until the fish is cooked and the top is brown. You may add a little more wine and water if the liquid seems to disappear too rapidly. You have to judge this for yourself; it is impossible for me to say exactly since I do not know the size and thickness of your fish.

6. If the pineapple seems too large for just two people, cut it in half and wrap one half in waxed paper and keep it in the

refrigerator. Place the half you are going to use cut side down on a chopping board and hold it either by the top leaves or by pushing a fork into the center of the bottom part. Remove the skin, cutting from the top of the fruit down. Be sure your knife is good, sharp, and long. With a small paring knife, cut out the "eyes," then cut the pineapple into slices or dice. Sprinkle it with a very little sugar and chill well.

MARKET LIST: 1 can cream of chicken soup, curry powder, potatoes, paprika, parsley, chopped sweet pickles, onion, bottled green peppers, or 1 fresh green pepper, 1 small can pimento, frozen asparagus, fillet of fish, 1 pineapple.

YOU SHOULD HAVE ON HAND: salad oil, butter, salt and pepper, dry white wine, bread crumbs, powdered sugar, tarragon vinegar.

That sour cream should be used up too, and although this dish does involve another onion, it's worth it.

Hamburgers Stroganoff
Cabbage and Dill Salad
Biscuits
Honey

1. Remove the outer leaves from a small head of green or white cabbage—not the purple kind—and cut the cabbage in half. Then quarter one of the halves and cut out the hard center core. Save the remaining half of the cabbage for use another time. Cut or chop the quarters of the cabbage into coarse flakes; you will have approximately 4 cups of cabbage, which is plenty. If the cabbage is a large one, use only one quarter of it.

Buy a ½-pound package of American processed cheese, sliced, and divide it in half. Put the unused half in the lower part of your refrigerator. Cut the cheese into thin strips (julienne). Cheese and butter are easier to cut if you wrap the blade of your knife in a sheet of waxed paper.

Add the cheese to the cabbage, which you put in a salad bowl, and lightly mix together.

Measure ¼ cup commercial mayonnaise into a measuring cup and add 1½ tablespoons French dressing, ¼ teaspoon salt, freshly ground pepper, 1 teaspoon sugar, ½ teaspoon Worcestershire sauce, and 1 teaspoon dill seeds. If you are fortunate enough to have, or are able to get, fresh dill, mince enough of it to make 1 teaspoon or add as much as you think you may like. Stir the dressing, pour it over the cheese and cabbage, mix well, and serve.

2. I suppose biscuits are the bride's class stumbling block. They need not be. I'm sure you can't miss on these. I'm giving you the full recipe because you can mix it all and put half in the refrigerator, or have some toasted for breakfast tomorrow. This will make about 20 medium biscuits.

Preheat the oven to 475°; depending on your oven, this will take approximately 10–15 minutes.

Sift together 2 cups all-purpose flour. To sift flour, put a measuring cup on a piece of waxed paper and sift the flour into the cup. Do NOT SHAKE the cup to check your measurement. Level the flour off gently with a spoon. It is important not to pack the flour down.

Now, add 3 *level* teaspoons double-acting baking powder and 1 teaspoon salt to the flour and resift this mixture into a bowl.

Pour into a measuring cup, but DO NOT STIR TOGETHER: ⅓ cup cooking oil, ⅔ cup milk, then pour all at once into the flour. Stir with a fork until the mixture leaves the sides of the bowl and rounds up into a ball.

Turn the dough out onto a sheet of waxed paper, knead it gently (lightly) once or twice by turning the dough over and pressing down with the heel of your hand and pushing the dough away from you.

Pat or press the dough out to ¼-inch thickness, or roll out between sheets of waxed paper. Cut with an unfloured biscuit cutter and transfer to an ungreased cookie sheet (a plain, flat sheet of aluminum), brush the tops with a little cream, and bake 10–12 minutes. You *must* use all-purpose flour and the double-acting baking powder for this recipe. You may make "drop" biscuits by just dropping about a tablespoon of the dough onto the cookie sheet.

3.   Have your butcher grind 1 pound good beef, either top or bottom round.

Slice 1 onion thin.

Add to the hamburger 1 beaten egg, 1 teaspoon prepared mustard (that is, mustard that comes in jars and is wet; the other kind is dry mustard and comes in little cans), 1 teaspoon salt, ½ teaspoon black pepper (pepper comes black AND white), 1 tablespoon Worcestershire sauce, and 2 teaspoons butter, melted. Mix all this together and form into cakes.

79

Put a little butter, margarine, or oil into a skillet—I can't tell you precisely how much, it depends on the size of your pan; enough to thinly cover the bottom of the skillet, anyway.

Put the sliced onion in the pan together with the meat cakes. Don't have too high a flame—a medium fire is best because onions burn fairly easily; brown the cakes on both sides, remove them to a hot platter, and keep warm.

Lower the flame and make a sauce in the skillet (pan), with the onion still in it, as follows:

Melt 2 tablespoons butter, sprinkle with 2 tablespoons flour, and stir in until well mixed, using a wooden spoon. When the flour and butter are light brown (NOT burned), pour in 1 cup meat stock (either 1 bouillon cube dissolved in 1 cup hot water or 1 cup canned bouillon) slowly whilst you stir.

Add 1 teaspoon prepared mustard, 1 teaspoon soy sauce, ½ cup tomato catsup, and ¾ cup sour cream, also 2 tablespoons Sauce Diable, which is a bottled sauce procurable at a fancy grocery. It's not essential, but it's nice, or you may substitute HP sauce.

Simmer this sauce for 5 minutes; that is, cook it just under the boiling point. You can add a little minced parsley to it just before you pour it over the hamburgers. Don't let this stand too long; the sooner eaten, the better.

MARKET LIST: 1 pound ground beef, 2 cans bouillon, catsup, Worcestershire sauce, 1 jar mustard, Sauce Diable or HP sauce, soy sauce, honey, small cabbage, dill seeds, American processed cheese, sliced.

YOU SHOULD HAVE ON HAND: onion, egg, pepper, salt, butter or margarine, sour cream, flour, cooking oil, double-acting baking powder, olive oil (for French dressing), tarragon vinegar, milk, mayonnaise, sugar.

*This can be a very fancy dish if you like, but it is also very simple,
satisfying, and cool.*

Chutney Canapés
Veal Chops in Jelly
Green Salad Parmesan
Blueberry Shortcake

1.   Soak 2 tablespoons gelatin in ¼ cup cold water in a bowl.
The gelatin will look very strange and granular, but don't worry
—it is all right. Add 4 tablespoons malt, wine, or tarragon vinegar
to the gelatin and mix together.

Heat 2 cans consommé and pour this over the gelatin and
stir until the gelatin is dissolved. If you have any white wine
handy (dry is best) you might add about ⅔ cup to the consommé when you are heating it.

Pour about ¼ inch of this gelatin mixture into a shallow glass
dish of a size that suits the chops and put the dish into the
refrigerator so that the layer of gelatin will chill.

Trim the excess fat from four rib veal chops, about ½ inch
thick. (Don't forget to wipe the chops off with a damp cloth.)

Put 2 tablespoons butter or margarine in a frying pan and,
when the butter is sizzling-hot, put in the chops and cook them
on both sides until they are golden brown. Sprinkle them with a
little salt and pepper as they are cooking. Lower the flame, cover
the pan, and continue cooking the chops for 30 minutes more.
When they are done, remove them from the pan and drain them
on paper toweling or brown paper.

When the gelatin is set, arrange the cooked and cooled chops
on top of the layer of jelly and pour the remaining gelatin mixture over the chops, covering them well.

If you are energetic you may dress up this dish by arranging
slices of cooked carrots and sliced, stuffed olives, or quartered
artichoke bottoms, canned or freshly cooked, on top or around

81

the chops. Or, if you have leftover, cooked, frozen mixed vegetables, you may sprinkle some over and between the chops. Don't put the chops too close to the edge of the dish, leave enough space so that they will be entirely surrounded by the gelatin.

This dish may be served either in the glass dish or unmolded —I advise the former method at this moment in your culinary career. Put the dish back in the refrigerator or freeze to jell.

2. Buy one half of a pound cake and split in half.

Heat the leftover blueberries and pour some between the layers of the cake and some on top.

A little whipped cream, if you like it, will dress this up a bit.

3. With a small, sharp knife, cut the end out of a head of lettuce in a deep, circular motion and let cold water run through it. This should separate the leaves.

Cut the end off of a head of escarole or chicory and wash the leaves. Tear both greens into pieces, wrap in a towel, pat as dry as possible, and put in the refrigerator.

When you are ready to serve the salad, put the greens in a wooden bowl, sprinkle with 3 tablespoons grated Parmesan cheese, add French dressing, and mix well before serving.

This recipe poses two problems: A, the French dressing; and B, GARLIC.

French dressing is an investment in time as it will keep for ages in a covered jar. You make it thusly:

¾ cup olive oil
4 tablespoons malt, wine, or tarragon vinegar
¾ teaspoon salt
Freshly ground pepper

Combine all ingredients in a small jar and mix well. Cover and store.

As to the garlic, garlic is a bulb, a lily bulb, and each "head" of garlic is composed of several "toes," also known as cloves. Break off one toe of garlic, remove the white papery covering, cut off both ends of the toe, and peel off the brown inner skin. You have now peeled a toe of garlic. Cut the toe in half and rub the inside of your salad bowl with the peeled garlic, then drop the remains of the toe or clove into your French dressing. Be sure that it doesn't slip out when you pour the dressing over the salad.

4.   Trim the crusts from 2 slices of white bread; with the aid of the top from a large can, you can cut rounds out of the slices —a slightly dressier touch. Fry the bread in a little previously heated butter (about 2 teaspoons) and drain on a paper towel.

Spread the toast with deviled or potted ham and then with chutney. Chutney is a condiment, a combination of various fruits, herbs, and spices, and comes in a bottle.

Sprinkle with a little grated Parmesan cheese and set in a 375° oven for 5 minutes to brown.

MARKET LIST: 4 rib or loin veal chops ½ inch thick, butter, 2 cans consommé, 1 box plain gelatin, vinegar, bread, salad material, potted ham, chutney, grated Parmesan cheese, garlic, pound cake, whipping cream.

YOU SHOULD HAVE ON HAND: salt and pepper, oil, vinegar for French dressing, leftover blueberries.

Scalloped Sea Food
Rice
Sliced Beet Salad   French Dressing
French Bread
Honeydew Melon

1.   You have already cooked rice and you probably made enough French dressing yesterday to have enough for today.

2.   The salad may be made with fresh or canned beets. Canned beets are very good and using them is a great timesaver. Instead of sliced beets, you might prefer the tiny baby beets. Arrange the vegetable on a leaf of lettuce, pour French dressing over it, chill and serve.

3.   Cut the melon in half and remove the seeds with a spoon. Chill, and serve with a quarter of lime or lemon. Some people like a little powdered sugar to sprinkle on.

4.   Put ½ quart water into a pot and season with ½ teaspoon salt and a good dash of cayenne pepper. Add ½ pound fresh or frozen shrimp and boil 7–10 minutes, or until pink. Drain, cool; remove shells, heads, legs, and the black vein.

Pour boiling water over ½ pound scallops in a pot, let them simmer for 3–5 minutes, and then drain.

You will need about 9 or 10 oysters. Be sure there are no bits of shell amongst them.

Mince enough parsley to make 1 tablespoon.

Squeeze enough lemon to make ½ tablespoon.

In a saucepan, melt 2½ tablespoons butter, then add an equal amount of flour and stir.

Slowly add 1 cup warm milk, stirring the while, and keep on stirring until thickened and smooth.

Now add the parsley, lemon juice, and salt and pepper to your taste, and 1½ teaspoons Worcestershire sauce. Mix.

Stir into this sauce the various prepared sea foods.

Pour the whole thing into a buttered casserole, cover with nicely buttered bread crumbs, and bake in a preheated 425°–475° oven for about 8–10 minutes, or until bread crumbs are well browned and the contents of the casserole are hot and bubbling.

5.   Slice the French bread part way through, spread soft butter or margarine generously between the slices, and put it on a cookie sheet or pan in the oven with the casserole about 5–10 minutes before serving.

If you want garlic bread, mince 1 clove garlic very, very fine and then mash it a bit with the flat of your cleaver. Mix the garlic with the softened—not melted—butter, and spread between the slices of the bread.

MARKET LIST: 1 small can beets, French bread, honeydew melon, ½ pound shrimp, or 1 can shrimp (wet pack), ½ pint oysters, parsley, lemon, milk, butter, Worcestershire sauce, lettuce, ½ pound scallops.

YOU SHOULD HAVE ON HAND: flour, French dressing, rice.

I'm trying to avoid too expensive meat dishes, but after all, life is hardly bearable without a steak every once in a while, so here goes:

Steak
Frozen French Fried Potatoes
French Spinach
Pound Cake with Chocolate Sauce

1. It's quite possible that you won't want any dessert except coffee, but you can use this some other time. Buy ½ pound of pound or "sunshine" cake (so help me!) and some already-canned chocolate syrup. Slice the cake and pour the heated (or unheated) sauce over the slices, or pass the sauce separately.

2. Cook the frozen French fried potatoes according to the directions on the box.

Sprinkle the potatoes with a little salt when they are done.

3. Cook the contents of 1 box frozen spinach according to the directions. Drain in a colander, pressing the water out with a wooden spoon and mashing the spinach a bit.

Put as much butter as you feel you can afford—up to 4 tablespoons or as little as 2 tablespoons—in a skillet or saucepan. Let the butter get hot and foamy, and then add the spinach, mix, mash, and add salt and pepper. Cook just long enough for the butter to mix well with the spinach. A dash of nutmeg is a nice finishing touch.

If you want to make the dish a little more dressy, you may garnish it with quartered hard-cooked eggs or triangles of white bread which have been fried in butter until a lovely, golden brown.

For creamed spinach, proceed as above, using only 1 or 2 tablespoons butter. When the butter has got to the foamy stage, add 1 teaspoon flour (sprinkle it on the butter) and mix briskly. Add the spinach, mix well, and cook a few minutes. Season with salt, pepper, and nutmeg. Add ½ cup HOT milk, mix well, bring to a boil, and cook for a few more minutes.

4. Your groom may want to cook the steak, but in case he is not so inclined, here is what you do. Buy a porterhouse, T-bone, pin-bone sirloin, or minute (individual) steak. The meat should be dark red and have veins of white fat running through it. Count on ½ pound per person and get it thick rather than long. Remember that the bone is considered in the weight. Wipe the meat off with a damp cloth, trim off the surplus fat, and save 1 piece of fat to grease your pan or broiler. If you are using your broiler, preheat it for about 10 minutes, put your steak in the center of the broiling rack, and place it so that the top of the meat is about 1½ inches from the flame. Sear, turn, and sear on the reverse side. For steak 2 inches thick and rare, broil 22-25 minutes, for medium, 26-30. If you use a pan, grease it and heat it to sizzling-hot. Sear the meat—that is, cook it quickly over a high flame on one side, then, with a pancake turner, flip the steak over on the other side; this is done to keep the juices from running out. Sprinkle with salt and freshly ground pepper, then turn, repeat so that the meat is seared and seasoned on each side, then *cooked* on each side. Lower the heat a little and cook approximately as for broiled steaks. Of course, smaller steaks take less time. Place a slice of butter on top of the steak when it is finished. Deciding just when a steak is cooked is a difficult matter. Experience will teach you, but in the meantime, it may be necessary to cheat just a little; make a small incision in the meat and peek; you can tell from the color whether or not the steak is done to your taste.

MARKET LIST: steak, frozen French fried potatoes, frozen spinach, pound cake, chocolate syrup.

YOU SHOULD HAVE ON HAND: butter or margarine, salt, pepper, paper towels, milk, nutmeg.

By this time perhaps you feel confident enough to tackle a chicken. I'll give you two simple ways of doing a fowl, and you may take your choice; also, you can serve it either hot or cold.

Roast Chicken
String Beans
Canned Baba au Rhum

1. Buy a packaged, frozen chicken since it is already drawn and "dressed" (a contradictory description, as the bird is obviously completely naked; but the term means that the feathers and insides have been removed and that the chicken is cleaned and prepared for cooking). However, examine the chicken well, and if there are any pinfeathers remaining, pull them out with tweezers. Pinfeathers look almost like splinters under the skin of the chicken. Roasting chickens come about 3½–5 pounds—naturally you don't want one that is too big, but it should be large enough so that you will have some left over for tomorrow. Use an uncovered roasting pan for all poultry and roasts, and be sure to use the metal thing at the bottom of the pan which is known as a trivet or rack. It is usually a flat object with holes in it. Make a note of how much your bird weighs—this is very important as you must gauge your cooking time by weight.

Defrost the chicken; this takes quite a long time, so allow plenty of it.

Remove the bag from the inside of the chicken, which contains the giblets.

Season the inside of the bird by rubbing it with ⅓ teaspoon salt. Tie the wings together with a bit of string or kitchen thread. Leave the string on the legs.

Rub the chicken all over with ½ lemon and, with a small brush or some waxed paper, brush the whole bird with oil (not olive) or melted margarine.

Put it in the roaster, breast side up ON the trivet or rack that comes with the roaster, and arrange 2–3 pieces of bacon over the breast. Roast as follows:

2–3 pounds	325°	72 minutes per pound
3–4 pounds	325°	50 minutes per pound
4–4½ pounds	325°	43 minutes per pound
Capon	325°	35 minutes per pound

Put the bird in the preheated oven and do nothing more—it will take care of itself. You just figure out the cooking time. The chicken is roasted when, if it is tipped toward its tail end, the juices run out clear.

Remove bacon and cook debaconed for the last ½ hour. Carving the bird is another problem entirely; perhaps your spouse can handle that.

2. If no one wants to—or can—carve, try doing the chicken this way: buy 2 halves of a broiling-sized chicken or have one cut in half.

Treat it with oil or margarine, as you would the roasting chicken. Mix a little salt and pepper together and sprinkle this on the inside part of the halves, then put them in a small baking pan, skin side up. (A baking pan is a shallower pan than a roasting pan.)

Bake in 400° oven for 25 minutes, then turn them over, fill the halves with ready-made stuffing, using only half the amount and prepared according to directions on the package. Brush again with oil and bake about 30 minutes longer. At this point I must urge you to get—if you do not already own—a pair of kitchen tongs; they are indispensable for turning and lifting things.

When the chicken is done, remove it to a hot platter and proceed with the gravy.

3. Technically, the giblets are the heart, liver, gizzard, and entrails. I am happy to say that when you buy a frozen or dressed and drawn bird the latter have been, or are, removed, together with the gall bladder, lungs, kidneys, crop, and windpipe. Only the giblets are kept and used.

With a small, sharp knife, cut away any veins or membrane there may be from the heart.

The gizzard has a tough outer muscle surrounding an inner sac; carefully cut through the outer casing and remove this sac, being careful not to break it. Throw this away. The liver is all right as it is. Wash the giblets in cold water.

4.   Put the heart and gizzard—not the liver—in a little saucepan and cover them with water.

Add 1 stalk celery, cut into 2 or 3 pieces, and 1 small onion, peeled and sliced. Cover the pan and allow the giblets to simmer until tender; approximately 35 minutes.

Now, add the liver and about ½ teaspoon salt and continue cooking for 25 minutes more. Let the stock cool.

5.   Pour the liquid from the roasting pan into a jar or measuring cup, measure 2 tablespoons of it into the roasting pan, and place the pan over a burner with the flame turned very low.

Add 2 tablespoons flour to the hot fat, mix well together, and stir constantly. Allow to cook until brown.

Then add 1 cup of the cooled giblet stock and stir the gravy until it is smooth and thick. Season and add the chopped giblets.

6.   Cook the frozen string beans according to the directions on the box.

Drain the beans and either return them to the saucepan to keep warm or put them in a serving dish. Pour over a little melted butter.

7.   The canned baba may be served hot or cold. Follow the directions on the can.

MARKET LIST: 1 frozen chicken, 1 box frozen string beans, 1 can baba au rhum, small jar mayonnaise, packaged poultry stuffing, lettuce.

YOU SHOULD HAVE ON HAND: margarine (or oil), salt and pepper, bacon, lemon, flour, celery, onion.

If you had a fair-sized roast chicken, you should have enough left over for dinner tonight. And if you feel energetic you could also make a chicken soup to have either tomorrow or the next day—it's better made the day before.

Chicken Hash with Noodles
Russian Salad
Popovers

1.   Cook 1 box frozen mixed vegetables, drain and chill.

Mix together 2 tablespoons bought mayonnaise, 2 tablespoons French dressing, 2 tablespoons chili sauce, and a little Worcestershire sauce.

Mix the dressing with the vegetables and serve either in a bowl lined with washed, dried lettuce leaves and garnished with slices of hard-cooked egg, or on lettuce on individual salad plates.

2.   Don't be afraid to try these popovers. I put them in because it's fun to have a surprise in your menu, and these really pop!

Sift, then measure, and sift again 1 cup plain flour (not self-rising or cake flour) with ¼ teaspoon salt.

Break 2 eggs into a bowl and beat lightly.

Stir 1 cup milk and 1 teaspoon melted butter into the eggs.

Add (meaning pour in gradually, not all at once) the egg-butter-milk mixture to the flour and stir until well mixed and smooth. You may use your electric beater if you like.

Grease 4–6 custard cups—4 large or 6 smallish—and fill them slightly more than half full of the batter.

Put the half-filled cups on a cookie sheet and place them in a COLD oven. Light the oven and set it at 425°. Bake the popovers for 1 hour. You'll be surprised!

3.   Break the noodles in pieces about 1½ inches long and enough to make 2 cupfuls. Bring 2 quarts water, to which 1 teaspoon salt has been added, to a boil in a deep pot.

Add the noodles slowly, trying to keep the water boiling.

91

Cook them without the top on the pot. Stir frequently with a fork. Test for doneness in about 10 minutes. If they are tender and yet still firm when bitten into, they are done.

Drain in a colander and rinse with cold water.

You may reheat them or keep them hot in a double boiler over hot water.

Add 4 tablespoons melted butter to the noodles and a little pepper. Mix lightly.

4.   Cut enough meat from the leftover roast chicken, both white and dark meat, to make about 1 or 1½ cups meat. Be sure to remove any small bones or other unattractive bits.

Heat the meat in a saucepan in 1 cup heavy cream. If you have more than a cup of meat, use a little more cream.

Let the cream and chicken reduce, that is, cook down to about half. Add a little salt and perhaps a dash of Worcestershire sauce if you like. Combine noodles and chicken mixture, and serve at once.

5.   Here is the recipe for chicken soup if you did not use the giblets for gravy. You really should use up that carcass and the objects in the little bag that came from the interior of the frozen chicken.

Put into a deep pot (the kind of utensil without a handle is generally referred to as a pot in contrast to cooking containers with long handles, which are known as saucepans) the remains of the chicken, the carcass, that is, which has been cut into pieces with your shears after you have removed from the bird in one way or another all the meat you can.

Cover with water, about 4 cups, and add ¼ teaspoon salt. Put the cover on the pot and simmer for 1 hour.

Then add 1 cup clean celery leaves, 1 sliced onion, ½ cup sliced carrot, 3 sprigs parsley, and the chicken giblets. Simmer all this until the liver is tender—poke it with a fork to ascertain same. If it is cooked, remove it; we'll deal with it later. Continue simmering for 1 hour more.

Remove the giblets from the soup and chill.

Strain the soup through a wire strainer lined with a piece of cheesecloth, and either return it to the refrigerator for future use or heat and eat. When you serve the soup, add the little pieces of meat you took from the bones.

MARKET LIST: 1 box frozen mixed vegetables, 1 small jar mayonnaise, 1 six-ounce package broad noodles, ½ pint heavy cream.

YOU SHOULD HAVE ON HAND: French dressing, chili sauce, Worcestershire sauce, lettuce, celery, parsley, carrots, onion, flour, milk, butter, eggs.

*I'm including fish dishes because even though you may not par-
ticularly care for fish, still it varies your menus, and there may
be times when you may want it.*

Salmon and Artichoke Bottoms in Sour Cream
String Bean and Potato Salad
Mixed Frozen Peaches and Black Cherries

1. If you have some leftover string beans, use them (proportions of beans to potatoes should be about ⅓ potatoes to ⅔ string
beans); otherwise, cook frozen string beans according to directions
on the box. Drain.

Boil 2 small potatoes (unless you want to cook more and save
the unused potatoes for tomorrow).

Cool the potatoes, peel them, and cut up coarsely.

Wash 1 small green onion, cut off the top and root, peel off the
outside layer, and chop. At the same time chop a little parsley.

Mix the beans and potatoes, onions and parsley together, pour
on some French dressing, and chill. A little prepared mustard
could be added to the dressing you use on this salad.

2. Buy the kind of cherries that come in a jar—get the small-
sized jar and mix with 1 package defrosted peaches. Pour a little
kirsch liqueur over this. This—as all fruit desserts—should be
ice-cold.

3. Take a small- to medium-sized baking dish, either ovenproof
glass or the heat-resisting china kind, grease it well with cooking
oil or butter.

Drain 1 can artichoke bottoms and put them in a pan with a
little heated margarine or butter and cook them lightly. Arrange
them on the bottom of the baking dish and season.

Canned artichoke bottoms are not always procurable; instead,
you may use previously cooked (see page 72) fresh artichoke
bottoms. Remove the choke, discard the leaves, and trim the
bottoms neatly.

Open and drain 1 large can salmon, remove any bit of skin or bone, and flake, or, in other words, separate the salmon into thin, small pieces. Cover the artichoke bottoms in the baking dish with the flaked salmon.

Pour 1 cup sour cream evenly over the whole business and brown in a 325° oven. Lemon quarters are nice served with this. The artichoke bottoms may be omitted entirely; proceed as indicated, adding ½ teaspoon dry mustard to the sour cream before pouring it over the fish. Bake at 400° for 20 minutes.

MARKET LIST: 1 large can salmon, 1 pint sour cream, 1 jar artichoke hearts or bottoms, 1 package frozen string beans, 1–2 pounds potatoes, frozen peaches, Bing cherries.

YOU SHOULD HAVE ON HAND: green onions, parsley, margarine or butter, salt and pepper, lemons, French dressing, prepared or dry mustard, kirsch liqueur.

This recipe makes 4 cups of soup, but since it is your main course and should be served in large, deep soup bowls or casseroles, I am giving the full amounts.

Egg Canapés
Goulash Soup
Western Salad
Frozen Viennese Cream

1.   Melt 24 marshmallows in ¾ cup hot strong coffee. Cool. Whip ¾ cup heavy cream and mix together with the coffee and melted marshmallows.

Pour this mixture into a shallow glass serving dish—or a mold if you like—and freeze. About 2 hours in a freezer—4 hours in a refrigerator. (See **HOUSEHOLD HINTS** for unmolding directions.)

2.   Toast 2 slices of bread.

Snip a small amount of the following (about ½ teaspoon each): parsley, chives or green onion, and enough celery to make approximately 1½ tablespoons.

Mix all these together and mash well with the contents of 1 small can tuna fish—drained of its oil. Spread this combination on the toast.

Poach 2 eggs, drain if necessary, and when they are cool, place them on top of the tuna mixture.

Very gently, in order not to injure the eggs, cover them with a thin layer of mayonnaise. Chill.

3.   One pound beef, round or rump. Wipe it off and cut it into medium to smallish cubes.

Also peel and cube 4 medium-sized raw potatoes, peel and chop 3 medium-sized onions and slice 1 peeled medium-sized tomato. To peel a tomato, have some water boiling in a small saucepan and let the tomato stand in it for 2 or 3 minutes, take the tomato out and let it cool a bit, then carefully make an incision in the skin and you will find it peels off readily. Tomatoes will slice and scoop out better if they are chilled after peeling; however, for this soup you needn't be so fussy.

Measure a quart of water into a good-sized pot, add 1 teaspoon salt, a little pepper, the meat, and onions. Simmer until meat is nearly done. Be sure you bring the water to a simmer before you start counting time. Add potatoes and sufficient water to make one quart of soup. Simmer 10 minutes.

Add the sliced tomato and 1 teaspoon Hungarian paprika and simmer over medium to low heat until the meat is tender.

Right here I would like to give a little dissertation on the use of salt in cooking. Salt is a mineral; it remains when the food and liquids reduce and cook away, therefore don't overdo salt in the beginning of your cooking, especially in soups—you can always add it just before the end.

Take about ¼ package wide noodles and drop into 2 cups rapidly boiling salted water (¼ teaspoon salt). Cook about 9 minutes. A couple of teaspoons of oil added to the water will help prevent the noodles from sticking. When they are tender, (test them by the tooth method), pour them into a colander, and run cold water over them for a few seconds. Add the noodles to the soup a few minutes before serving.

4. Prepare ½ cup toasted croutons (little cubes of bread, toasted or fried).

Mash 1 small bud, toe, or clove of garlic slightly and put it in a covered jar with 2 tablespoons salad oil and set aside.

Core, wash, and dry 1 small head lettuce or ½ head and break the leaves into pieces. Prepare 1 small head or a few leaves of chicory the same way.

Mix 3 tablespoons salad oil with 1 teaspoon Worcestershire sauce, ½ teaspoon salt, a little freshly ground black pepper, and ¼ cup crumbled blue cheese (similar to Roquefort cheese).

97

Mix this lightly into the greens and then break one raw egg on top of the whole thing.

On top of the egg, pour 4 tablespoons (¼ cup) lemon juice (strained). Toss well.

Dip the croutons in the garlic oil, from which you have removed the garlic, add them to the salad, and toss some more.

If you still have those chicken livers, a truly lavish touch is to sauté them gently until thoroughly cooked, then crumble them up over the salad just before the last tossing. Magnificent!

MARKET LIST: 1 pound beef rump or round (top or bottom), 4 potatoes, 3 onions, 1 tomato, Hungarian paprika, noodles, lettuce, chicory, lemons, bread, small amount blue cheese (about 1/8 pound), 2 dozen marshmallows, ½ pint whipping cream, small can of tuna fish, parsley, green onions, celery.

YOU SHOULD HAVE ON HAND: eggs, salt and pepper, salad oil, garlic, Worcestershire sauce, coffee, mayonnaise.

If you made that chicken soup the other day, you may use it for this dinner; otherwise, you can make this with canned chicken broth—that is, clear chicken soup without rice or noodles.

Onion Canapés
Petites Marmites
Chicken Livers in Red Wine
Water Cress Salad
New Potatoes
Apricot Pie

1.   This soup should be served in individual casseroles, also called *marmites*. You want about 2 cups chicken broth, to which you add 1 small onion, sliced, 4 tablespoons (or ¼ cup) of either leftover, canned (and drained), or fresh de-podded peas and one small carrot, scraped and sliced.

Simmer everything together until hot, or, until the vegetables are tender. If you had any leftover slivers of chicken, put them in too.

Pour the soup into the *marmites,* float a thin, thin slice of French bread, with the crust, on top of the soup, sprinkle the bread with grated Parmesan or other Italian cheese, and place in a moderately hot (400°) oven, or under the broiler, for 2 minutes without the lids on the *marmites* or until the cheese is brown.

2.   You, TOO, can make a pie. At least you can try, and I'd be willing to bet you can make a very decent crust with this simple recipe. If worst comes to worst, you can eat just the apricots. Here goes:

Preheat your oven to 425°.

Sift first, then measure 2 cups all-purpose flour, 1½ teaspoons salt, and sift into a bowl.

Measure in a measuring cup, but DO NOT MIX, ½ cup vegetable oil and ¼ cup cold milk.

Pour the oil-milk combination into the flour all at once. Stir

A DELICIOUS dough for turnovers is made by combining a cup of flour with half a cup of butter and from three to four ounces of cream cheese.

99

with a fork until slightly mixed, round the dough into a ball, and —if you are going to make a 2-crust pie—divide it in half. In this case, leave it all in 1 ball and flatten it slightly.

Place the dough between 2 sheets of waxed paper and roll out gently. Roll the dough away from you, lifting the rolling pin as you reach the rim of the dough. If the bottom paper wrinkles, turn the whole thing over and roll on the other side. Turn the paper frequently in order to roll the crust evenly. Gauge the size of the pastry by holding your pie plate over it, allowing about 2 inches extra. This will be taken up by the depth of the pie pan and the edge of the pie. Your pie plate may be either heavy aluminum or ovenproof glass. An 8–9 inch pan is a good size. If you use a smaller pan, as you might just for two, use only half the pastry and freeze the balance.

Peel off one of the waxed papers. If the dough breaks, press the edges together or press a scrap of pastry lightly over the tear. Lift the paper with the pastry sticking to it and turn it paper side up into a pie pan.

Gently remove the paper and work the pastry down into the pan. With kitchen shears, trim the overhanging edge about 1 inch from the rim of the pan, fold it outward and under, and press it onto the rim of the pan with the prongs of a fork. With the fork, prick the bottom of the pie shell all over, including the sides. This keeps the pie shell from shrinking.

For a 1-crust pie, bake it for 8–10 minutes; if you are making a 2-crust creation—filled—bake it 40 minutes, or until golden.

Check the pie as it is baking; many ovens cook "hotter" in the back, and you may find your pie is done in the rear and not so done in the front. Take two pot holders and turn it around and continue cooking. Remove it from the oven when the crust is done.

In my early pie-making days I found that the amount the experts used to make a 2-crust pie was barely sufficient for me to make a 1-cruster, such was my clumsiness in rolling out pastry. You may find the same thing; in which case, be not discouraged, just use the whole amount of pastry, and eventually experience will enable you to make 2 crusts when you are supposed to.

Now, drain a can of apricot halves—try to buy the kind that are peeled—and tastefully arrange the fruit in the bottom of the baked pie shell. You should have about 1½ cups fruit.

Mix together: ¼ cup heavy cream (that means whipping cream), 1 tablespoon granulated sugar, 1/8 teaspoon powdered cinnamon, the gratings of 1 lemon, and 2 beaten egg yolks. We have now come upon two problems: A, grated lemon. Wash the lemon and scrape it up and down on a medium grater. You won't get much lemon, but it will be enough, especially if you remember to scrape off the bits that stick to the back of the grater. Grate the lemon onto a piece of waxed paper. B, egg yolks. BE SURE THE EGGS ARE FRESH. If you are uncertain, break them one at a time into a little saucer—then one unhappy egg won't spoil the good ones. So break the egg into a saucer and with your fingers quickly fish out the yolk. This sounds ghastly, but I assure you it is much the simplest and easiest way to separate eggs. Let all the white, or as much as possible, dribble off the yolk, and put the yolks into the bowl with the cream, sugar, cinnamon, and lemon. (Another method of separating eggs is to break the egg into a small funnel; the white will drip through and the yolk remain in the funnel.)

Beat this mixture for about 2–3 minutes with an electric or a rotary beater; the latter is the kind with a hand-operated wheel at one side which operates two beaters.

Pour this custard over the fruit in the pie shell and bake in a 325° oven about 15 minutes, or until the custard is set. That means that when you pierce the custard with a knife the knife will come out clean. Serve the pie hot or cold—I prefer the latter.

3. Buy about 12 of the tiniest new potatoes you can find and scrub them well. In a heavy iron skillet heat 1 or 2 tablespoons butter or olive oil and put the potatoes in the pan, shake the pan

well in order to cover the potatoes with the oil. Place a cover on the pan and cook them very slowly, shaking the pan from time to time until they are tender. Poke one gently with a fork to ascertain doneness. I can't give any definite time for cooking because this depends upon the size of the potatoes.

4. Peel an onion and cut into as many slices as you will require canapés.

Cut an equal number of bread rounds and put a slice of onion on top of each.

Spread generously with mayonnaise and sprinkle with a little grated Parmesan cheese.

Put the canapés on a cookie sheet or in a shallow pan and place in a preheated 350° oven until the mayonnaise "souffles." Serve piping-hot.

5. Finely chop 1 shallot.

Mix with ¼ cup red wine.

Cut 6 fine chicken livers into halves.

Put 1 tablespoon butter into a skillet and melt over a low fire.

Add the cut-up chicken livers to the hot melted butter, turn the fire up a bit, and sauté the livers for about 5 minutes. Test by pricking with a sharp knife and remove whilst they are still pink in the middle. Remove them temporarily from the skillet, but be sure to leave the wine mixture in the pan.

Let this wine-butter juice combination cook down to half of its original volume, then add ½ cup canned consommé.

Let this come to a boil, and then reduce the heat and allow just to simmer until only three quarters of the original amount remains. (If you have pots and pans that have the measurements shown on the sides, this is a great help.)

While the sauce is simmering, brown 6 little mushroom caps in butter.

With your kitchen shears, cut up enough bacon into tiny squares to make a scant ¼ cup. Have a little water boiling in a saucepan, add the bacon bits, and boil for 3 minutes. Drain.

When the sauce is properly reduced in the skillet, add the bacon and mushrooms. Mix together and season with salt and pepper, remembering that the bacon is salty, so not much salt will be needed.

Add the partially cooked chicken livers to the sauce, together with a few snips of parsley—enough to make about ¼ teaspoon. Allow to cook just a minute or two whilst gently mixing together, then serve.

6. Wash 1 bunch water cress in cold running water. Then separate the bunch in a colander or sieve and remove any brown or mashed branches.

Place the prepared water cress in a salad bowl and keep it in the refrigerator until you are ready to serve.

Pour a very small amount of French dressing over the water cress and toss lightly.

MARKET LIST: new potatoes, 6 chicken livers, 1 bunch water cress, 1 bunch shallots, 1 small can mushroom caps, all-purpose flour, cooking oil, powdered cinnamon, 1 can peeled apricot halves, lemon, whipping cream, 1 small can peas, consommé, French bread.

YOU SHOULD HAVE ON HAND: butter or oil, bacon, red wine, eggs, milk, waxed paper, sugar, onions, Parmesan cheese, mayonnaise, French dressing.

If your bank account is in a healthy condition, you might treat yourself to steak again. Try getting the small club or individual steaks—not too thin, about 1 inch thick.

Little Steaks
Sort of Refried Beans
Bermuda Salad
Gingerbread

1. Remove the outer leaves and the stalk from 1 small head of cauliflower. Break or cut off the flowerets, that is, separate the little stalks that make up the whole cauliflower. Soak these for ½ hour in salted water (2 tablespoons salt to 1 quart water). Drain and dry.

Core and wash lettuce. Break into pieces and dry.

Peel and slice thin ½ large Bermuda onion—the purple kind.

Slice enough stuffed olives to make approximately ½ cup.

Crumble 2½ ounces blue or Roquefort cheese.

You may add water cress too. Wash the water cress and cut off a little of the stems and discard any bad leaves. Shake dry.

Put this entire collection in a large bowl, and add just enough French dressing to coat the salad. Toss lightly.

2. Start the beans a good bit before the steak—they'll keep anyway.

Drain 1 can kidney beans and save the liquid.

Heat ⅓–½ cup bacon drippings in a heavy (meaning iron) skillet (frying pan).

Add some of the beans and mash well (I use a potato masher). Add more beans and mash; add some of the liquid from the beans and continue until you've used up all the beans and the liquid. Keep on cooking over medium-high flame, stirring and mashing frequently until the beans are thick and dry. I cook this in a shallow copper pan and serve the beans in the same dish—saves washing one more utensil.

3. Prepare your meat as you did for the first steak menu. Pan-broil these. Get the pan sizzling-hot, rub with a little fat, and sear the steak quickly on one side and then on the other. Season with salt and freshly ground pepper. Turn again and cook about 6 minutes on each side, more if you like steak well done.

4. I have said earlier that I rarely use mixes, but I have found that the already mixed gingerbread is excellent and a cinch to do. Just follow the directions on the box.

MARKET LIST: 2 small steaks, 1 can kidney beans, 1 small cauliflower, 1 small head lettuce, 1 bunch water cress, 1 small bottle stuffed olives, small piece blue or Roquefort cheese, 1 large Bermuda onion (failing a Bermuda onion, the salad is perfectly all right with a yellow onion), gingerbread mix.

YOU SHOULD HAVE ON HAND: bacon drippings, French dressing, salt and pepper.

This is an easy one. The **Poor Boy Sandwich** *is a New Orleans institution, and if New Orleans had never produced any other gastronomical innovations it would still head the list with* **Poor Boy Sandwiches,** *the Dagwood par excellence, and* **Oyster Loaves.**

Poor Boy Sandwiches
or
Oyster Loaves
Baked Apples in Cream

1. Mix 2 egg yolks and 1 scant teaspoon flour with a fork until smooth.

Stir in ½ cup whipping cream, ¼ cup milk, 6 tablespoons sugar, 2 tablespoons of kirsch, and a dash of vanilla.

Wash 3 medium-sized apples, peel them, and remove the cores with a special instrument known as a corer. Push the corer into the stem end of the apple all the way through the fruit, pull it out with a turning motion. You should have the core intact inside the corer.

Put the apples in a small buttered or oiled baking dish. Pour the custard over the apples, sprinkle with a tiny bit of powdered cinnamon, and bake in a 350° oven for about 35–40 minutes. You may serve them either hot or cold.

2. If you cannot procure individual loaves of French bread, buy as small a size as you can and cut into pieces according to the state of your appetite. Then slice each piece into halves lengthwise.

Have some butter softened, or mayonnaise, and slather this on the halves of the bread.

Next, lay a few leaves of washed and dried lettuce on the buttered or mayonnaised bread, followed by 2 or 3 slices of tomato.

From here on out, anything goes. Usually there will be a layer of Swiss or Italian cheese, cold meat of any kind—beef, veal or ham, or any sort or sorts of sausage or canned meats. Sometimes some antipasto or mustard is spread over the completed arrangement just before the second piece of bread is applied to finish the sandwich.

3. The **Oyster Loaf** is similar in construction.

Use the same French bread and cut as you would for the above **Poor Boy.** Only this time brush the halves generously with melted butter and toast very, very lightly.

Fish about 12 oysters out of a pint jar of "loose" oysters; examine them to be sure there are no bits of shell clinging to them.

Melt ½ stick butter and, with a fork, impale the oysters one by one through the tough, roundish muscle, and dip each one in butter and then in bread or cracker crumbs, to which you have added a little salt and some pepper.

As you complete each dipping process, place the oyster on a buttered or oiled cookie sheet.

Light your broiler and have a medium to high flame.

Place the sheet with the oysters under the flame—not too close—and broil them, turning them often. Oysters should not be cooked too much or they toughen.

When the oysters are plump and done, arrange them on one half of the French bread and place the other half on top.

Oyster loaves are classically served with catsup and chopped pickles.

Of course, the oysters may be fried in deep fat, but deep-fat frying is rather a tricky operation and perhaps better left until you are a more experienced cook.

MARKET LIST: individual loaves of French bread or 1 loaf of a larger size, lettuce, tomatoes, cheese, cold meat or sausage (if you haven't sufficient leftovers), mustard, antipasto, 3 cooking apples, ½ pint whipping cream, eggs.

YOU SHOULD HAVE ON HAND: butter or mayonnaise, flour, sugar, kirsch, vanilla, cinnamon, milk, bread or cracker crumbs.

107

How about tackling a veal roast? Cooking a large piece of meat is really the simplest of all cooking, and by far the most economical in time and fuel consumption; also, you have leftovers—another desirable angle.

Roast Leg of Veal
Brussels Sprouts   Roast Potatoes
Raspberry Mousse

1.   Mash 1 box defrosted frozen raspberries thoroughly, add some granulated sugar to taste—you may not think they need any—and chill them.

Whip 1½ pints whipping cream with ½ teaspoon vanilla, and fold in (that means to add the whipped cream gradually to the mashed fruit), turning the mixture over and over away from you gently in a circular motion.

Chill thoroughly in the freezing unit, or in a bowl in the refrigerator. It will take about 4 hours in the refrigerator, about 2 hours in a freezer. In any case, this can be made far ahead of time. You may put this in a fancy mold if you like, but at this point I advise either freezing it in a refrigerator tray or a bowl and scooping it out. This can also be made with frozen strawberries or peaches.

2.   The best veal to buy for roasting is the leg. About 3 pounds will give enough for leftovers.

Wipe off the meat and place it on the rack (or trivet) in the roasting pan. Be sure to remember how much the roast weighs so that you can gauge the cooking time. Lay several strips of bacon or thin slices of salt pork (ask your butcher for the latter) over the meat after you have judiciously seasoned it with salt and pepper. PUT NOTHING ELSE IN THE PAN. NO BASTING IS NECESSARY. Bake UNCOVERED in a 325° oven 25–30 minutes to the pound. If you have a meat thermometer—and I recommend one highly —use it according to directions. It should register 180° or higher if you like the meat well done. If not, the veal is cooked when the gravy in the pan is brown. Place the roast and the potatoes (see below) on a well-warmed platter, turn off the heat in the oven, and put the platter in the oven to keep hot while you make the gravy.

Strain the liquid from the roasting pan into a measuring cup and let it cool. This process may be hastened by placing the cup and its contents in cold water. The fat will rise to the top.

Scoop off 2 tablespoons fat for each cup of gravy that you wish to make. Take off the rest of the fat and store in the refrigerator (this is drippings) but keep the balance of the liquid in the cup.

Put the fat back into the roasting pan, sprinkle in 2 tablespoons flour. Place the pan over very low heat and carefully and thoroughly stir the flour into the fat. Keep stirring and stirring; the well-browned (NOT burnt) flour and fat will impart a rich brown color to the finished product.

If you have less than 1 cup of liquid left in the measuring cup—and there is probably not that much remaining, add canned bouillon to make up the difference.

Very, very slowly stir this liquid into the flour-and-fat mixture in the pan. Keep on stirring until the mixture is smooth. It should be allowed to boil gently.

Season with salt and pepper, and you may, if you wish, add a little bottled condiment sauce to your taste. There are especially made coloring and seasoning agents available which may be added if the gravy is not of a rich enough color.

3. Peel and put into cold water for 15 minutes small uniform-sized potatoes. Drain and dry them with paper towels.

Put the potatoes in the pan with the roast about 45 minutes before the roast is supposed to be done. Baste them often with the drippings in the pan. Use a glass or metal baster—and save many oven burns.

4. Cook the frozen Brussels sprouts as the directions on the box indicate.

109

Drain well and place them in a serving dish that can be kept hot. Pour a little melted butter over them.

MARKET LIST: veal roast (leg)—about 3 pounds, 1 pound potatoes, 1 box frozen Brussels sprouts, bacon or salt pork slices,
frozen raspberries or strawberries, 1½ pints whipping cream.
YOU SHOULD HAVE ON HAND: paper towels, sugar, butter, salt and
pepper.

If you roasted the veal yesterday, you should have ample left over for tonight's dinner. There are many ways of preparing leftover veal, but after all, one aim of this book is to make things as easy as possible, so why not just have the veal cold?

Hot Egg Hors d'Oeuvres
Cold Roast Veal
Baked Potatoes
Garden Salad

1.   You may prepare this hors d'oeuvre well ahead of time. If you want to be dressy about it you can cut circles out of stale bread with a large biscuit cutter or the top of a baking powder can and fry them lightly in foamy butter until golden brown—don't forget to drain them on a paper towel. If you don't want to bother with the bread circles, cut the crusts from 2 slices of bread and fry them.

Hard-cook 3 eggs, shell and chop them fine.

Mix with 2 tablespoons grated cheese 2 tablespoons finely minced green pepper, ¼ teaspoon salt, and a dash of cayenne pepper.

Dilute some mayonnaise with half as much melted butter (or margarine).

Combine the dressing with the egg mixture and spread this quite thickly on the fried toast. Put this in the oven for a minute or two before serving.

2.   Choose your potatoes as nearly the same size as possible so that they will cook in the same length of time. Scrub them well and dry. Brush each one with a little oil, prick each with a fork, and put the potatoes on a small baking sheet in a hot (450°) oven. Bake about 45–60 minutes, or until tender.

Take them out of the oven at once and make a smallish crisscross cut across the top of each potato to let out the steam. Hold

111

the potato in your hand in a dish towel and press it from the bottom so that the inside part pops out through the cut.

Top with a generous slice of butter, a little salt and a dash of paprika, and serve right away.

3. Rub a salad bowl with ½ small, peeled clove of garlic.

Discard the outer leaves of a head of lettuce and remove, wash, and dry about 6 leaves.

Wash 1 small cucumber and, with a sharp table fork, score it, that is, run the fork from one end of the cucumber to the other, cutting deep tracks. Now, slice the cucumber thin. If you are a person to whom this particular fruit behaves in a treacherous manner, soak the cucumber in ice water. Drain and dry before adding to the salad.

Wash 4 radishes, cut off the tops and the roots, and slice.

Deseed 1 green pepper and cut into thin, thin strips. If you have a shredder, use it. Don't forget to remove the white veins.

Scrape 2 large ribs of celery after cutting off the leaves, and dice.

Slice a half dozen or so stuffed olives. You may mix this all with plain French dressing, or French dressing to which you have added a little tomato catsup and prepared mustard to taste, or some dried herbs; either basil, savory, or dill (about ¼ teaspoon to ½ cup dressing).

MARKET LIST: bread, 2 green peppers, salt, cayenne pepper (in small cans), 1 pound potatoes, lettuce, 1 cucumber, 1 bunch radishes, 1 head celery, small jar stuffed olives.

YOU SHOULD HAVE ON HAND: eggs, mayonnaise, butter or margarine, cooking oil, French dressing, garlic.

This is supposed to be "quick" chili; I can't say it's so very fast, but it cooks by itself for quite a while, so that you should have time to recover from your efforts.

Quick Chili
Corn Bread
Cole Slaw
Fresh Cherries

1.   Ask your butcher to grind 1 pound lean beef. You don't HAVE to have the best, but if it is to be really lean ask for top or bottom round.

Melt 2 tablespoons fat—which may be any shortening, i.e., creamed vegetable shortening, butter or oil, lard or suet (suet is the fat of beef)—in an iron Dutch oven or a casserole over low heat. Actually, though, bacon drippings are the best of all for this particular dish.

Chop 1 large onion, mince 1 clove garlic, and shred (that means the thinnest "sticks" possible) 1 green pepper. Cut the pepper in half lengthwise, remove veins and seeds, and shred the pepper the long way, not in rings. Put these in the hot fat, cover, lower the heat, and fry gently for 10 minutes. Onions and garlic can burn quite easily, so give them an occasional stir. Don't let them brown.

Now, add the ground meat, increase the heat, and cook, stirring all the time until the meat is brown—about 1 minute (that doesn't mean *dark* brown).

Add the contents of 1 drained can kidney beans and lower the heat.

Mix 2 tablespoons (at least) chili powder in ¼ cup cold water in another pot.

Combine this with 1 cup drained, canned tomatoes (save the juice).

Add 1 bay leaf, 1 teaspoon salt, and a dash of cayenne pepper.

113

Bring all this to a boil, and then pour it over the meat and beans.

Cover closely and simmer on top of the stove for ½ hour. Or, if you have cooked the chili in a Dutch oven, pour into a greased casserole, cover, and bake in a 375° oven for 45 minutes. Personally, I use a large casserole; I find it works very well and saves cleaning an extra pot. Serve in *marmites* or bowls.

About chili powder—as with curry powder, we never seem to get a really good, hot chili powder, so if you like the taste of chili, use your own judgment and add more to taste.

2. Shred 1 very small cabbage or half of one. To shred, cut the cabbage in half and with a sharp knife continue cutting vertically, making slices as thin as you can. A gadget called a shredder may be bought—it is frequently combined with a grater. I advise procuring one.

Crisp the shreds in ice water, drain them, and mix them with ½ pimento, chopped, and any dressing you may fancy; French or sour cream are both good.

Whip ⅛ cup sour cream and add 2 tablespoons vinegar, ½ teaspoon paprika, ⅛ teaspoon salt, and perhaps 1 teaspoon sugar. Snipped chives are a lovely addition. Mix everything together, and then mix with the cole slaw. Remember all salads should be cold, cold, cold.

3. Wash the cherries—1 box is plenty—and remove the stems unless you like to eat them just as is in your fingers.

If you feel like being fancy about your dessert, you may cook the cherries in red wine—in this case, cut off half of the stems, put the cherries in an enamel saucepan, and pour over them 1 cup good red wine, add 1 *stick* cinnamon (it comes 2 ways, powdered and in sticks—usually available anywhere) and ½ cup sugar.

Cook on a very low fire for 10 minutes. Add a little more wine if you think it is needed.

Fish the cherries out, using a slotted spoon or slotted "turner" so that the juice drips back into the pan and arrange the fruit in a serving dish.

Return the juice to the fire and let it cook down (reduce) over a low flame until it is quite thick.

Add 1 tablespoon currant jelly, and when the jelly has melted, remove the cinnamon stick and pour the sauce over the cherries and serve the whole dessert very cold.

4. Very good corn bread mixes may be bought, but I prefer the homemade variety. Take your choice.

Heat your oven to 425°. Take a heavy iron pan or skillet (it should be on the small side so that the corn bread will be quite deep) and grease it generously with butter, oil or, preferably, bacon drippings. Put the greased pan in the oven and let it get sizzling-hot.

Sift together ¾ cup flour, 3 teaspoons baking powder, 2 tablespoons granulated sugar, and ½ teaspoon salt.

Add ¾ cup yellow corn meal.

Break 1 egg into a bowl and beat it well.

Add to the egg 3 tablespoons bacon drippings (or melted butter) and ¾ cup milk, and beat well.

Pour the egg-milk mixture into the flour-corn meal mixture, and mix very quickly, combining the ingredients just until the mixture looks rather lumpy.

With a well-padded pot holder, and taking care not to let your arm come in contact with the hot oven, pull out the rack on which you placed the pan or skillet and pour the corn bread mixture into it. Bake it for about 25–30 minutes.

To serve, cut into squares.

MARKET LIST: 1 pound ground beef, 1 can kidney beans, 1 medium can tomtaoes, chili powder, 1 small cabbage, 1 pint sour cream, 1 box cherries, 1 green pepper, 1 box stick cinnamon, currant jelly, 1 box yellow corn meal.

YOU SHOULD HAVE ON HAND: bacon drippings, garlic, onion, bay leaf, cayenne pepper, vinegar, paprika, salt, sugar, red wine, baking powder, milk, flour, 1 egg, granulated sugar.

115

This is a practically non-energy-consuming menu. I would have a hearty bread with it—Italian or French, for instance.

Crab Meat Piquante
Peas and Mushrooms
Coeur à la Crème with Raspberries
(or Strawberries)

1. As usual, I would take advantage of the frozen vegetables and cook the peas according to directions.

Try to find—and buy—the small, canned French button mushrooms. Mix a sufficient quantity of the mushrooms with the peas and some butter. Keep the vegetables hot.

Dried mushrooms are really mushroomier than the canned and very simple to use; they are used a great deal in Chinese and Italian cooking. Just soak a few of the dry, woody-looking objects in cold water until they soften—a matter of a few minutes. Drain and dry them, heat them thoroughly in a small pan with some oil, or butter, and then add to the peas—or whatever dish in which you wish to use them.

2. Try to buy the really fresh, *lump* crab meat. That means the big pieces of meat from the claws. Or, failing that, a good grade of canned crab meat. Avoid at all costs some brands of frozen crab meat that are on the market; the meat is tough, stringy, and salty.

Inspect the crab meat carefully for any bits and pieces of shell. Lightly pile it into small buttered casseroles, or if you have the very pretty scallop shells, use them.

While the crab meat is heating in a moderate oven, fry crisply 1 strip bacon for each serving, drain on brown paper or a paper towel, and place on top of the crab meat.

Mix well together the following: ½ teaspoon dry mustard, ¼ teaspoon paprika, a slight dash of Tabasco, ¼ teaspoon celery salt.

116

Then add ¼ cup regular bottled chili sauce and ½ teaspoon tarragon vinegar. Mix this concoction well.

Add not quite 1 cup mayonnaise, and mix.

With a spatula, spread the mayonnaise mixture over the warmed crab meat.

Have your broiler lighted and flame about medium. Place the crab meat in the broiler under the flame until it assumes a lovely glaze.

3. Traditionally, Coeur à la Crème is made in a heart-shaped wicker mold, but it may either be put in any mold you care to use or simply heaped in a small serving bowl and chilled.

With a silver fork, mash 4 ounces cream cheese and gradually beat in 4 tablespoons sour cream and ⅛ teaspoon salt. If you are using a wicker mold, wring out a small piece of cheesecloth in cold water before laying it against the inner surface of the mold, or lightly oil the mold. To unmold, see directions in HOUSEHOLD HINTS.

Defrost the berries, but keep them cold, and either surround the unmolded cheese with them or serve them separately.

You might also pour a little of that whipping cream you have over the cheese after you unmold it.

MARKET LIST: 1 box frozen peas, canned or dried mushrooms, ½ pound crab meat, dry mustard, paprika, Tabasco sauce, celery salt, chili sauce, tarragon vinegar, mayonnaise, bacon, 4 ounces cream cheese, sour cream, fresh or frozen raspberries or strawberries.

YOU SHOULD HAVE ON HAND: butter, or oil, paper towels.

Chicken Soup
Liver en Brochette
Braised Celery
Melon

1. You know how to prepare the melon. Do so, and put in the refrigerator to become well chilled.

2. Buy celery with crisp, green leaves—for this dish the white celery is best. (The green celery—Denver—is best for serving with raw carrots or as an hors d'oeuvre.) Remove the leaves, wash well, and also remove any discolored parts with a sharp knife. The small, delicate stalks in the inside of the celery should be removed and served as above. The leaves should be used as flavoring in soups or stews. Cut off the root part of the stalk and discard.

After removing the leaves and the root part of the stalk of celery, cut the head lengthwise, making about 4 pieces.

In a wide skillet, melt 2 tablespoons butter, then add the celery.

Next, add a bit of beef stock (or consommé). Cover the pan with a lid, lower the flame, and allow to simmer very gently for about 20 minutes. Season with salt and a tiny bit of white pepper.

Take the cover off the pan and place the pan in a 350° oven and allow to cook, basting frequently, until almost no liquid remains. When you serve the celery, pour some of the sauce over it.

3. Calf's liver is the best—and likewise the most expensive. Beef, pork, and lamb's liver are less expensive and, although full of nutritious substances, not quite as tasty. One pound of calf's liver is almost enough for 4 people; therefore you may judge accordingly—probably about ½ pound will be enough. Buy ½-inch slice.

Wipe the liver with a damp cloth, dry, and peel off the outside skin and remove tubes (if any).

Cut the liver into squares of about 1½ inches.

Snip bacon into as many squares as you have pieces of liver.

Quarter, and then cut into smaller sections, 1 tomato.

Ditto with 1 onion.

118

Cut in half and then remove the seeds and veins from 1 green pepper. Next, cut the pepper into squares about the size of the liver squares.

Now, you need 2 skewers. Skewers are simply pointed pieces of metal (heavy wire) with a twist at one end which forms a sort of handle. Or, you may use a shishkebab type of skewer; these usually have a wooden handle and are much more attractive than the ordinary skewer. Thread the prepared meat and vegetables on the skewer, alternating the liver, onion, pepper and bacon squares. You may also add mushroom *caps,* as your fancy dictates.

Over a low flame, heat a little bacon grease together with a few bits of bacon.

Put the brochettes into the pan with the hot bacon and let them cook for about 3–5 minutes, turning them often.

Remove the pan from the fire and place it in a preheated oven (450°), or under the broiler, until the meat is tender. It should be still pinkish in the center.

4.   You know how to do the chicken broth too.

MARKET LIST: ½ pound calf's liver, 1 can chicken broth (if desired), 1 large green pepper, 1 large tomato, mushrooms (if desired), 1 melon, 1 bunch white celery, 1 large onion, skewers.

YOU SHOULD HAVE ON HAND: Consommé, salt, pepper, bacon, bacon fat, butter.

I think it's about time for a party. This one can be prepared as far ahead as you like and you can appear before your company as though you had never set foot in the kitchen. You may omit the soup, if you like; it just depends on how elaborate you want to be —also how many dishes you want to face later.

Jellied Borsch

Cold Broiled Chicken   **Tomato Indienne**

Frozen Rolls

Strawberries Romanoff

1. Drain the juice from 1 large-sized can beets and put to one side.

Mash enough of the beets—either with a potato masher or in an electric mixer—to fill 1 cup.

Combine the mashed beets with the beet juice, together with 2 cups canned bouillon.

Add 2 tablespoons chopped onion and simmer gently for 4–5 minutes.

Add 2 tablespoons red wine vinegar and ½ teaspoon salt.

Dissolve the contents of 1 envelope of plain gelatin in ¼ cup cold water and stir this into the soup. Chill for several hours.

Serve in cold soup cups with a bit of sour cream on top of each serving. Snipped chives or a little black caviar may go on top of the sour cream if you are feeling very fancy.

2. For this, you may buy either ½ broiler for each person or just the breast. I prefer the latter; nothing discourages me more than to have to cope with a whole half of a chicken.

Wipe the pieces of chicken off with a damp cloth, and this time do not remove the skin.

Mix a little salt and pepper together and rub into each piece lightly.

Place the pieces in a pan under the broiler, skin side down. Cook until they are brown under quite a hot flame, turning them

120

often. Use your kitchen tongs for this operation. They will take about 20 minutes to cook.

Remove and let the chicken cool slightly, and then spread each piece generously all over with prepared mustard, English, if possible.

Prepare bread crumbs (*please* don't use the bought kind), and dip each piece of chicken into or cover it with the crumbs.

Sprinkle a little melted butter over the chicken and return it to the broiler.

Cook until golden brown.

To serve, place the chicken pieces on thin slices of trimmed ham —Virginia is best, but plain already-cooked ham will do. Garnish your platter with curly parsley. This dish may be either hot or cold.

Serve with the following sauce: Mix ½ cup bottled chili sauce with ½ teaspoon Worcestershire sauce, ½ teaspoon finely chopped chives and parsley.

3. If you don't feel equal to coping with hollowing out tomatoes for this salad, just put the rice in a bowl and surround it with slices or quarters of tomatoes; or make a mound of the rice on a glass dish and garnish it the same way.

However, to hollow a tomato, proceed thusly: skin the tomato and chill. Slice off the top. With a sharp spoon, and proceeding with extreme caution (you don't want to tear the skin), scoop out the seeds and insides of the tomatoes. Sprinkle with a little salt and place them upside down on a plate or platter and put them in the refrigerator to drain for about 20 minutes.

Cook 2 cups (to serve six or seven) of rice and cool.

Dice ½ green pepper and ½–1 pimiento.

Make a dressing of 3 tablespoons olive oil, the juice of 1 lemon, ½ teaspoon salt, a dash pepper, ½ teaspoon curry powder, and 1 tablespoon chutney.

Mix the sauce with the rice, and either stuff this into the tomatoes or serve as I suggested at the beginning of the menu. Garnish your salad with lettuce and/or water cress.

121

4. Buy 2 boxes fresh or frozen strawberries. If the berries are fresh, remove any spoiled ones and pull the hulls, or green part, from the balance; wash them, and sprinkle with (preferably) powdered sugar.

Whip ½ pint (bought) vanilla ice cream slightly.

Whip ½ pint heavy cream until stiff and fold into the ice cream.

Add the strained juice of 1 lemon, 2 ounces (6 tablespoons) Cointreau, and 1 ounce (3 tablespoons) Bacardi rum. Pour this over the strawberries. Combine with the ice cream mixture. Place dessert in the refrigerator until it is to be served.

5. I forgot about the rolls; as usual, follow the directions on the box. They are the only nearly last-minute thing you will have to do.

MARKET LIST: broilers, prepared mustard, slices of ham, curly parsley, No. 2½ can diced beets, 2 lemons, 2 cans bouillon, plain gelatin, 1 small jar caviar, tomatoes, rice, 1 green pepper, small can pimiento, chutney, lettuce, water cress, 2 boxes strawberries, 1 pint vanilla ice cream, ½ pint whipping cream, Cointreau, Bacardi rum (light), frozen rolls, butter, chives or green onions, red wine vinegar, curry powder.

YOU SHOULD HAVE ON HAND: stale bread for crumbs, sour cream, salt and pepper, onions, chili sauce, Worcestershire sauce, olive oil, sugar.

If this is a party, you had better order extra ice and check your soda water.

You may have some chicken left over from your party that you would like to use up, and there may be other odds and ends as well; so why don't you have them for dinner and ONE *hot dish:* **Cheese Soufflé?** *Everyone seems to panic at the thought of soufflé. There are three tricks—your oven must not be too hot, you must eat it* IMMEDIATELY, *and to insure against any possibility of failure, add 1 tablespoon of practically any spirituous liquor (including gin!) to the mixture before you add the egg whites. The taste of the liquor evaporates and the alcohol makes the soufflé puff up.*

Party Leftovers
Red, White, and Green Salad
Cheese Soufflé

1. Cook the frozen Lima beans as per directions on the box.
Peel and chop fine (mince) 1 small onion or ½ onion.
Wash, cut off the roots and tops of 3 radishes, and dice them.
Mix vegetables together and chill. Serve with French dressing.
2. Melt 4 tablespoons butter or margarine in the top of a double boiler, add 4 tablespoons flour, and blend with a wooden spoon.

Have 1½ cups milk heated and add this slowly to the butter-flour, together with 1 teaspoon salt and a dash of cayenne pepper.

Cook until the mixture is smooth and thick, stirring constantly. (This is a medium white sauce.) Don't be alarmed if the sauce is lumpy at first—keep on stirring and all will be well.

Have ready ½ pound (2 cups) packaged American (processed) cheese cut into small pieces.

Turn the heat off under the double boiler and stir in the diced or broken-up cheese. Continue stirring until the mixture is smooth.

Separate 6 eggs. (See p. 101.) Beat the yolks until frothy and gradually add them to the cheese sauce—stirring all the time until well mixed.

123

Cool. (You see, you can do this ahead of time—only don't let the mixture get absolutely cold—and then proceed with the remainder 1 hour before dinner.)

Beat the egg whites until stiff. Don't expect this to happen in an instant—it takes a few minutes. They are stiffly beaten when they make very glossy peaks that stand up when you withdraw the beater.

With a fork or spoon, fold the beaten whites into the cheese-egg mixture. Don't worry if there are a few small globs of egg white "unincorporated"; pour the whole thing into an UNgreased casserole and bake 1 hour in a SLOW (300°) oven.

If you have a small casserole, you may cut this recipe in half. Check the soufflé during the cooking time—a smaller one will take a shorter time.

MARKET LIST: 6 eggs, ½ pound processed American cheese, milk, frozen Lima beans, radishes.

YOU SHOULD HAVE ON HAND: salt and pepper, cayenne pepper, flour, margarine or butter. You should have sour cream left over from yesterday; onions, French dressing.

Spaghetti with meat sauce has many things in its favor, not the least of which is the use of a minimum of pots.

Sidney's Antipasto
Spaghetti with Meat Sauce
Baked Peaches with Liqueur Sauce

1.   This recipe makes a very generous amount of antipasto, but it keeps well, and then there may be more than just the two of you for dinner.

Grate the contents of ½ small can tuna fish with a fork.

Add the contents of 1 small can (preferably) skinless and boneless whole sardines, 1 scant cupful drained, canned tiny peas or leftover beans, 1 large raw carrot, diced—having previously cut off the root and stem ends and scraped it—4–5 sweet pickles that have pickled cauliflower among them.

In addition, if you like them, put in a dozen drained capers.

Make the dressing as follows: Mix together 2½ tablespoons garlic vinegar with 3 tablespoons olive oil and ½ can Sauce Arturo —NOT tomato paste.

Pour the dressing over the tuna fish, etc., and mix well with a large spoon. Chill.

2.   Pour ½ cup olive oil in a deep casserole and add 2 cloves minced garlic, 5 sliced onions, and brown slightly.

Add: 1 large can tomatoes, 1 can Italian tomato paste (contents only), 2 bay leaves, 1 teaspoon sugar, salt and pepper.

If you think you would like fennel, which has a licoricy taste, you may add 2 teaspoons powdered fennel at the same time.

Cook SLOWLY for 1 hour.

Now, add ½ pound chopped or ground beef, stir the mixture, and cook for another ½ hour. Be sure this cooks slowly. If the sauce gets too thick, add a little more tomato paste.

One pound of spaghetti will serve 6 people, so you want only

125

½ pound. There are various sizes of spaghetti—thick and thin. Use a large pot and lots of water.

If you are cooking half the pound of spaghetti, put 1½ teaspoons salt in the water and the same amount of butter or margarine. The fat will prevent the spaghetti from sticking. Bring the water to a rapid boil and lower the spaghetti into it.

After it has cooked about 12–15 minutes, watch to see that it does not overcook. Test it by biting into a strand; it should be firm but not tough.

Dump the spaghetti into a colander and run cold water over it for a few seconds. Now, you can put the spaghetti either on a warm platter or into a casserole; in either case, pour the meat sauce over it and have some grated Italian cheese ready to serve with it.

3. Buy a small can of peach halves. Put them in a shallow pan and fill the centers with a little maple syrup.

Bake them in a 375° oven for about 15 minutes.

Transfer them to a serving dish and pour over them a little whiskey, brandy, or sherry. If you like whipped cream, you might have some ready to pass separately.

MARKET LIST: 1 large can tomatoes, 1 can Italian tomato paste, 1 can Sauce Arturo, ½ pound chopped or ground beef, 1 pound spaghetti, 5 onions, 1 small can peach halves, 1 head celery, 1 small bunch carrots, 1 lemon, grated Italian cheese, maple syrup, whipping cream, celery, salt, 1 small can tuna fish.

YOU SHOULD HAVE ON HAND: olive oil, mayonnaise, salt and pepper, bay leaves, sugar, butter or margarine, brandy, sherry, or whiskey.

This is another of those Meal-in-one soups—really a potage of no mean proportions.

Cold Mixed Hors d'Oeuvres
Red Bean Soup
Cheese Board

1.   This is the time to use that hors d'oeuvres tray you received as a wedding present. There is almost no limit to the things you can use for cold hors d'oeuvres. Here are a few: sliced hard-cooked eggs mayonnaise, cold string beans with French dressing and snipped green onion bottoms, cold canned corn, any sort of sliced sausage or canned fish; tuna with chili sauce over it is good. Drain the tuna before you put it in the serving compartment. Cold, cooked, mixed vegetables combined with mayonnaise, pickled beets, canned pimientos, canned or bottled artichokes with French dressing, various sorts of olives, baked beans, shrimp mayonnaise, and so on, practically ad infinitum. Be sure everything is ice-cold. Chill the hors d'oeuvres in their little dishes in the refrigerator.

2.   In a large pot or casserole, melt 1 tablespoon bacon drippings or other shortening. Add the contents of 1 can red beans and heat.

Chop about ¼ green cabbage and put it in with the beans.

At the same time add ¼ cup uncooked elbow (short) macaroni. Cook 15 minutes.

Add 1 very small or ½ medium-sized onion, sliced, 1 clove minced garlic, 1 large diced potato, salt and pepper, a dash of paprika and a dash of cayenne. Cook 15 minutes more.

Add ½ can tomato sauce, 4 cups water, and 1 tablespoon strained lemon juice.

Mix and simmer until vegetables are soft and well done.

3.   Most imported cheeses taste better when eaten with fresh French bread and butter and with a little dry red wine to accom-

pany them. Cheddar, or "rattrap," cheese goes best with beer. Try different varieties of cheese; they are legion: French, Swiss, Scandinavian, German, Dutch, not to mention many lovely American cheeses. Unfortunately, the ordinary packaged cheeses leave a good deal to be desired; it is better to spend your money on the unpackaged kinds for a cheese board. Arrange one, two, or three different sorts of cheese on a cheese board or tray, surround with sliced French bread or crackers, and serve.

MARKET LIST: 1 can red kidney beans, 1 package macaroni, ½–1 small green cabbage, cold hors d'oeuvre material, cheeses, tomato sauce, French bread or crackers.

YOU SHOULD HAVE ON HAND: shortening or oil, salt and pepper, cayenne, paprika, garlic, potatoes, lemon.

Try to prevail upon your butcher to cut the meat for this dish for you. It may be difficult for you to make him understand you want the little strips really thin, about ½ inch wide and 3 inches long, but do your best. Be sure he cuts the meat across the grain; otherwise, it will be tough. You want good, lean beef for this, sirloin preferred.

Beef Stroganoff
Frozen French Fried Potatoes
Salade Chapon
Broiled Grapefruit

1.   Prepare a small head of lettuce, tearing the leaves into medium-sized pieces.

Take the end of a loaf of stale French bread—about a 3-inch piece—and rub it with a peeled, cut clove of garlic—as much or as little of same as you can stand. Tear the bread into small pieces and add to the lettuce.

Pour a generous amount of French dressing over the salad and let it sit until well fatigued—limp, that is.

2.   Sprinkle the meat with a mixture of salt and pepper and let it stand for about 2 hours.

Heat 2½ tablespoons butter in a pan and sauté the beef in it (with the cover on the pan) for about 12 minutes over a high flame, stirring the meat from time to time.

Slice ¼ pound either fresh or canned mushrooms and add to the beef; at the same time pour in ⅛ cup canned bouillon or stock made with a bouillon cube. (See directions on container of cubes for use.) Cook this mixture about 10 minutes.

Drain off almost all of the liquid before you transfer the meat to a double boiler, with the water in the under part boiling.

In another pan, heat 1½ tablespoons butter and cook 2 teaspoons minced onion in it until it just begins to change color.

129

Stir in 2 teaspoons flour and ⅔ cup sour cream, bring slowly to the boiling point, and add 2 teaspoons tomato paste.

Blend this combination together and pour over the meat and mushrooms in the double boiler and cook for 10 minutes more.

3. You've done the French fried potatoes before. The directions are on the box.

4. Cut a grapefruit in half and loosen the sections with a sharp knife. Take out the seeds and cut out the core with your kitchen shears, or a gadget that is especially made to do this.

Sprinkle each half with a tablespoon or so of brown sugar and put under a medium flame in your broiler, or bake in a hot (450°) oven until the sugar becomes runny.

When the halves are hot, spoon 1 tablespoon sherry over each and serve immediately.

MARKET LIST: 1 pound lean beef, 1 small can mushrooms or 1 box of fresh, canned beef bouillon or bouillon cubes, 1 onion, sour cream, frozen French fried potatoes, lettuce, 1 grapefruit.

YOU SHOULD HAVE ON HAND: butter or margarine, flour, tomato paste, dry mustard, brown sugar, sherry, stale French bread, French dressing, garlic.

I do hope you tried making that pie crust; if not, by all means do so now because **Tarte Lorraine** *is a lovely luncheon, buffet, or Sunday night supper dish.*

Clam and Tomato Bouillon
Tarte Lorraine
Artichoke with Butter Sauce
Canned Green Gage Plums

1.   Line a pie plate with the pie pastry; don't forget to prick the sides and bottom with a fork. You may also brush the edges with cream, using a pastry brush, to make it come out a lovely golden brown.

Lightly fry 4 strips of bacon, drain well on a paper towel, and crumble into small pieces.

Chop enough fresh or canned mushrooms to fill 4 tablespoons, and dice the same amount of Gruyère or a similar white cheese.

Also mince 1 tablespoon parsley and chop 1 medium-sized onion.

Sprinkle these combined ingredients in the bottom of your unbaked pie shell.

Beat 2 whole eggs in a separate bowl until slightly thickened and add 1 pint heavy cream, salt and pepper, and a dash of nutmeg. Stir this together and then pour it over the ingredients in the unbaked pie shell.

Bake the tart in an oven preheated to 325°–350° about 30–40 minutes. It should be golden brown on top, and should react properly to the custard test—that is, a knife inserted in the tart should come out clean.

2.   You know how to do the artichoke too. Only this time have it hot (be sure to drain it well) and serve it with melted butter, to which you have added a little strained lemon juice to taste.

131

3. Open a can of green gage plums, empty the contents into a crystal bowl, and chill.

4. The bouillon is made by diluting ½ cup tomato juice with a little water and then adding clam juice to taste. Clam juice comes already bottled. Chicken broth with oyster liquor added is another delicious, light soup.

MARKET LIST: Gruyère or similar-type cheese (the processed kinds will do), 1 small can tomato juice, ½ pound bacon, 1 small can mushrooms, 1 onion, 4 eggs, 1 pint heavy cream, nutmeg, parsley, artichoke, butter, margarine, 1 bottle clam juice, canned green gage plums.

YOU SHOULD HAVE ON HAND: flour, cooking oil, salt, lemon.

This dish has great merit, and not only because it takes care of itself—it tastes good, too. Put it on the stove and go on your merry way.

Beef in Red Wine
String Beans with Almonds
Rice
Brown Betty Tart

1.   Buy 1–1½ pounds top or bottom round of beef, depending on how you feel about your pocketbook and leftovers; wipe the meat and cut it into a dozen pieces after having removed the fat.

Brown 1 tablespoon butter over medium to low heat in a Dutch oven or heavy casserole. Put in the meat, turn the flame up to fairly high, add 2 sliced onions, and brown.

When the meat has browned, (seized) sprinkle it with 2 tablespoons flour and stir it around a bit.

Pour in 1 cup dry red wine and ½ cup water; add 1 teaspoon salt and ½ teaspoon pepper, and 1 clove peeled garlic, slightly bruised.

Cover the pot and bring the contents to a boil; lower the heat and allow to simmer for about 3 hours. If you can't keep it from boiling, put an asbestos mat under the casserole.

A bouquet garni is nice added just before you put the lid on; it is composed as follows: 1 sprig parsley, 1 sprig thyme, and 1 bay leaf. Tie these together with a bit of string or heavy thread, and fish it out before you serve the meat.

Just before serving, 'flambée' the beef by pouring ¼ cup warmed brandy or cognac over the meat and setting it alight.

2.   The rice you have cooked before; just follow the directions.

3.   Pare, core, and slice 4–6 apples, depending on the size of pie plate you intend to use. Arrange the slices in a pie plate and sprinkle with ½–¾ cup brown sugar. (When you measure brown

sugar, pack it well into the measuring cup; otherwise, you won't get the correct measurement.)

Mix together thoroughly ¾ cup more brown sugar, 1 cup plain flour sifted with ¼ teaspoon salt and ½ cup butter or margarine (1 stick of either), cut into bits, and about ¾ cup chopped nut meats (pecans or walnuts). Have the butter a bit soft and it will be easier to mix.

Spread this over the apples and press it down around the edge. Bake in a preheated moderate (350°) oven for 1 hour.

If you feel like going to the extra effort and expense of making hard sauce, it's very nice with this.

Beat ⅛ cup butter until light and creamy.

Add 1 cup sifted confectioners' sugar gradually whilst you continue beating (using an electric beater).

Add 1 teaspoon vanilla extract a bit at a time and a tiny pinch of salt.

Chill before using.

4. Buy only a small amount of almonds. If in shells, shell enough to fill 2 generous tablespoonfuls. Have a little water boiling in a small saucepan and drop the nuts into the boiling water. Allow them to remain 3–4 minutes. Remove the pan and drain off the water. You will find that the brown covering on the nut slips off readily with just a pinch.

Dry the nuts with a dish towel. With a sharp knife, cut them into slivers.

Heat 1½ tablespoons oil in a pan and add the nuts. Sauté them gently until they are golden. Remove and drain them on a paper towel.

5. After you have prepared the string beans, add the slivered almonds, mix lightly, and serve.

The amount of almonds given above is about right for ½ box frozen string beans.

MARKET LIST: 1–1½ pounds top round of beef, 2 onions, thyme

(this comes from the grocery store in a little bundle; it is dried), frozen string beans, rice, apples, ¼ pound pecan meats, almonds, confectioners' sugar.

YOU SHOULD HAVE ON HAND: Butter or margarine, flour, brandy or cognac, parsley, brown sugar, salt, pepper, lettuce, Tabasco, garlic, oil, dry red wine, bay leaf.

This **Baked Canadian Bacon** *does as well for a luncheon dish as for dinner; it's also very nice for a buffet supper, and for some reason or other, it is not often encountered.*

Jellied Chicken Broth
Baked Canadian Bacon
Frozen Succotash
Hot Blueberries

1. Buy 1 can plain chicken *broth,* not chicken soup with noodles or rice.

Soak ½ envelope unflavored gelatin in ¼ cup cold water for 5 minutes.

Heat the broth, then add the gelatin, and stir well.

Season with salt and pepper.

Pour into a bowl or into soup cups and put in the refrigerator to set.

2. The Canadian bacon comes either sliced or in one piece—for this, you want 1 pound all in one piece.

Put the bacon in a baking pan or roaster, uncovered, place in a preheated, moderate (350°) oven, and let it bake 35 minutes to the pound.

3. You should have room in your oven to cook the blueberries at the same time as the bacon. Or you may do them ahead of time and serve them cold instead of hot and with a little cream to pour over them.

Defrost 1 box frozen blueberries. Grease a small glass or oven-proof pie plate and fill with the berries.

Sprinkle with the strained juice of 1 lemon or 3 tablespoons bottled reconstituted lemon juice, 3 tablespoons sugar (taste the blueberries first, they may not need more sweetening), and a light sprinkling of powdered cinnamon.

Mix the following together until crumbly: 1½ tablespoons butter and ⅛ cup flour with 3 tablespoons sugar and a pinch of salt.

Sprinkle this mixture over the berries and bake in a moderate (350°) oven for about 30 minutes.

4. As usual, the succotash is cooked as per directions on the box. Drain and season before serving.

MARKET LIST: 1 pound Canadian bacon, frozen succotash, frozen blueberries, 1 bottle reconstituted lemon juice (if you want it) or 1 lemon, chicken broth.

YOU SHOULD HAVE ON HAND: Powdered cinnamon, sugar, flour, salt, gelatin.

I haven't said much about lamb chops because at this moment they are hair-raisingly expensive. Here are some veal chops instead.

Baked Veal Chops in Sour Cream
Noodles
Broccoli
Rum Cake

1. Buy loin or rib veal chops, as many as you feel you will need—or can afford—and have them cut about ¾ inch thick.

Wash and cut off the tops and roots of 4 green onions. Peel off the thin outer layer. Chop the onions coarsely and sauté them in a skillet over a low flame in 2 tablespoons hot oil or fat until golden.

Rub a little mixed salt and pepper on the chops (after wiping them off, of course), turn the flame up a bit, and sauté the chops quickly, browning them on both sides in the skillet with the onions. Pour over enough sour cream to practically cover them, put the lid on the skillet, and bake in a preheated moderate (350°) oven for 15 minutes.

Then lower the temperature to 250° and cook for an additional hour.

Take the cover off and let them brown—about 15 minutes.

2. Noodles are cooked in the same way as spaghetti. One cup of noodles will give you 1¼ cups after they are cooked.

Bring 2 quarts water, plus 1 teaspoon salt and 2 teaspoons oil, margarine, or butter, to a boil, and introduce the noodles slowly; let them boil about 20 minutes. Test them by the tooth method to see they don't get overdone.

Pour them into a colander and rinse with cold water.

Place the noodles on a warm serving dish or leave them in the colander and put the colander over a pot of hot water over a low fire, or in a warm oven with the door open until ready to serve. Rice is kept hot in the same way.

3. Cook the broccoli as the directions on the box indicate.

4. **Rum Cake** is another simple dessert made with a bought sponge cake.

Cut the cake in half horizontally and, depending on what you have on hand, sprinkle each half liberally with rum or brandy. Good, dark Jamaica rum is best, but any will do.

Whip ½ pint cream (heavy variety) until stiff, adding about ½ teaspoon vanilla whilst whipping.

Spread the cream between the layers of the cake. Place one layer on top of the first and cover the whole cake with the remainder of the cream.

Decorate it with pecan halves or chopped pecans.

MARKET LIST: loin or rib veal chops, sour cream, green onions, 1 package noodles, 1 box frozen broccoli, 1 sponge cake, ½ pint whipping cream, shelled pecans.

YOU SHOULD HAVE ON HAND: oil, or fat, salt and pepper, vanilla, rum or brandy.

This is a somewhat streamlined version of a famous Dutch soup; the original is made with dried split peas that have been soaked overnight and cooked with a ham bone—but this is an acceptable substitute, especially if you are in a bit of a hurry.

Dutch Soup
Egg and Onion Salad
Chocolate Cookies

1. In a double boiler, melt ¼ pound semi-sweet chocolate, either the chips or the squares.

Add ¼ teaspoon vanilla extract, ¼ cup chopped, shelled pecans, and 1 cup corn flakes. Mix together (over hot water) until everything is well blended.

Drop from a tablespoon onto a sheet of waxed paper which you have placed on a platter or cookie sheet and chill.

2. Add a dash of Worcestershire sauce to 4 tablespoons French dressing.

Peel and slice thin 2 onions, and put them in the dressing to soak for about ½ hour.

Hard-cook 2 eggs and slice them.

Place a lettuce leaf on each plate and arrange a few slices of egg on top of it, then some onion rings, and finally some more egg slices. Season with a sprinkling of salt and pepper, and pour French dressing over the salad.

3. Thin 1 can split pea soup with an equal amount of light cream.

Add about ¼ teaspoon sugar, ½ cup cooked (boiled) diced potatoes, and one frankfurter, sliced, per person.

Heat well together in a double boiler; do not allow to boil. Season. Serve in individual casseroles or bowls.

MARKET LIST: 1 can green split pea soup, ½ pint cream, 2 frankfurters, 1 green pepper, semi-sweet chocolate, 1 small box corn flakes, shelled pecans, onions, eggs, lettuce.

YOU SHOULD HAVE ON HAND: potatoes, sugar, vanilla, a little extra cream, French dressing, Worcestershire sauce.

Here is another New Orleans stand-by—with the famous sentence that begins almost all Creole recipes: "First, make a roux."

Shrimp Jambalaya
Russian Salad
Fresh or Frozen Peaches

1. Defrost the peaches and keep them in the refrigerator. Or, if you are using fresh peaches, peel them thin, cut in half and remove the pit, then slice the halves into medium-sized crescent-shaped slices. Sprinkle with a little lemon juice to keep them from discoloring, then some granulated sugar, and chill in the refrigerator.

2. Mix together thoroughly the following: 1 tablespoon mayonnaise, 2 tablespoons chili sauce, a little Worcestershire sauce, and one hard-cooked egg, sliced.

Defrost, cook, and chill 1 box frozen mixed vegetables.

Just before you are ready to serve, mix the vegetables and the dressing together; pile on a lettuce leaf in individual servings.

3. Wash the raw shrimp in cold water. Have ready 2 quarts boiling water, or enough to cover the shrimp, and add 1 generous tablespoon salt, or ½ tablespoon for each quart of water used. Let the water and shrimp come back to the simmering point, cover the pot, and let the shrimp cook until they are rosy, for about 15–20 minutes.

Drain the shrimp, save the water in which they were cooked, and run cold water over them. Peel off the shells and remove the heads and legs. Now is the time to take out the black vein that runs down the back of the shrimp. Use a sharp, pointed knife for the operation.

I think it is wise to prepare ahead of time all the minced, chopped, or peeled ingredients you will need (not only for this dish, but for any other). Therefore:

142

1 onion, chopped very fine
scrap of thyme, crumbled or finely chopped
½ bay leaf, crumbled or finely chopped
1 sprig of parsley, finely chopped
½ toe of garlic, finely minced
1 tomato, skin removed, chopped fine (with its juice)

Now, make a *roux*: In a good-sized pot or casserole and over a low flame, put ½ tablespoon butter, add the chopped onions, and stir for a moment.

Add ½ tablespoon flour and stir until well mixed.

Now, add the thyme, bay leaf, parsley, and garlic, and let this fry gently for about 4–5 minutes. Be exceedingly careful not to let the mixture brown too much and, above all, not to let it burn.

Add ⅛ teaspoon chili powder and the tomato and juice. Let this simmer about 8 minutes.

Bring 1 quart of the water you have saved from the shrimp to a boil. (If you haven't enough, add more plain water.) Add to the above.

Put the cooked shrimp into the boiling mixture and allow to boil for 3–5 minutes.

Add ½ cup uncooked rice, mix well, and boil for 20 minutes– ½ hour, stirring frequently to keep the jambalaya from sticking to the bottom of the pot. It should cook down quite a lot and be fairly solid, not soupy. If it gets too dry, add a little tomato juice, shrimp liquid, or water.

MARKET LIST: shrimp, mixed frozen vegetables, mayonnaise, frozen or fresh peaches, onion, lettuce, tomato, parsley, bay leaf, thyme, rice.

YOU SHOULD HAVE ON HAND: egg, chili sauce, chili powder, Worcestershire sauce, garlic, butter, flour, salt.

143

If you want to use this menu for a party, you may double the quantities in the recipes. The virtue of this salmon dish is that it requires NO *cooking, and on a hot day that might be quite an attraction.*

Cold Salmon Mousse
Beet and Water Cress Salad
Canned Crepes Suzette

1. Make the mousse well ahead of time so that it can become good and firm and you can relax.

MIXTURE A. Soften 1½ teaspoons plain gelatin in 2 tablespoons cold water.

Heat ½ cup consommé or bouillon and add the gelatin. Stir it until the gelatin dissolves.

Cut 1 peeled onion in half and scrape off about 1½ teaspoons. Mix with Worcestershire sauce, 1½ teaspoons vinegar, a little pepper, and 2 tablespoons minced pimiento. Chill well until thick.

MIXTURE B. Flake enough canned salmon to fill 1 cup.

Whip ¼ cup cream.

Dice very fine ½ peeled cucumber. (If the cucumber is small, young, and tender, you need not peel it.)

When the gelatin-bouillon mixture is thoroughly chilled, beat it well with an electric or rotary beater until it is frothy.

Fold the salmon, cucumber, and whipped cream into this.

Oil a smallish (1-pint-sized) mold, or rinse it out in cold water, and pour the mousse mixture into it. Needless to say, it must be chilled until very firm.

2. You may use cold, canned, sliced beets for this salad. Prepare some water cress and make a "bed" of it on your salad plates, or you may garnish the mousse with it. Arrange the beets on top and pour a little French dressing over them.

3. The canned crepes suzette have the directions on the can.

They may be served hot or cold and are very good with vanilla ice cream.

MARKET LIST: 1 large can salmon, 1 can consommé or bouillon, whipping cream, 1 small cucumber, 1 can or jar beets, 1 bunch water cress, 1 can crepes suzette.

YOU SHOULD HAVE ON HAND: unflavored gelatin, mayonnaise, onion, vinegar, salt and pepper, French dressing, Worcestershire sauce.

*Lagniappe: Extra Recipes

*New Orleanese meaning: a little something for nothing.

SOUPS

Clam Stew

Peel and slice 2 medium-sized onions; peel and dice 3 potatoes. Put these vegetables in a pot with just enough water to cover them and cook for 12–15 minutes.

Fry 4 slices bacon and drain on brown paper or a paper towel.

Grease a casserole and in it put the onions, potatoes, and bacon, and the contents of 1 large or 2 small cans minced clams.

Add 2 cups milk, a dash of nutmeg, and salt and pepper; put the cover on the casserole and place in a 350° oven for about 15–20 minutes. For two, as a main dish.

Father Williams' Onion Soup

For two people, peel and slice very thin 3 onions. Cook the onions slowly and gently in 3 scant tablespoons olive oil until tender but NOT brown.

Add 1 tablespoon butter, salt and pepper, and 2 teaspoons (or more) sugar. Cook a few minutes more over a very low flame.

Heat and add to the onions 2 cups consommé, bouillon or beef stock.

Toast 1 slice French bread for each person to be served; float it on top of the soup, which has been poured into *marmites,*

149

sprinkle generously with grated Parmesan cheese, and put the covers on the soup bowls. Bake in a 375° oven for 15 minutes.

Boula

This recipe will serve four generously.

In a double boiler, heat 1 can green pea soup mixed with 1 can clear green turtle soup.

When the soup is hot, add sherry to taste.

Whip about ¼ cup heavy cream, pour the soup into cups or, better still, into *marmites,* put a spoonful of whipped cream on top of each serving, and sprinkle a bit of grated Parmesan cheese on top of that.

Put the bowls under the broiler a moment until the cheese is lightly browned.

Crab Meat Mongol

This is another soup that is served in a *marmite* or individual casserole. See that the casseroles are hot before you pour in the soup.

Mix together 1 can condensed cream of tomato soup and 1 can cream of green pea soup.

Add 1 can bouillon and enough water to make it as soupy as you like. It should be fairly thick.

Add ¾ cup crab meat (preferably fresh); be sure the crab meat is free of any bits of shell, and heat well.

Just before you serve the soup, pour in a little sherry to taste. See that the soup is properly salted and peppered.

A dress-up touch is to pour about ¼ pint—or even less—of whipping cream into a bowl, sprinkle with a tiny pinch of salt, and whip it until stiff with a rotary or electric beater. Put a good spoonful or so on top of each serving of soup; put the bowls under your broiler and brown quickly.

Olives Add Zip to Soup

This quick and delicious soup, concocted from cans, has homemade flavor. Turn a can of condensed cream of chicken soup into a saucepan and add a cup of canned tomatoes, a pinch of chili powder, some chopped green onion and a generous half cup of ripe olive wedges.

Heat slowly to simmering, and serve topped with a sprinkling of grated Parmesan cheese. Ripe olives make an unusual and delicious ingredient in many soups.

MAIN DISHES

The Royal Roast of Beef

There are two ways of roasting beef. One in which the meat is seared at a very high temperature—500 degrees—for the first 15 minutes of cooking and then the oven temperature reduced to 350 degrees for the balance of the roasting period, and a second method whereby the meat is cooked at a constant temperature of 325 degrees. There are advantages to both methods. The first method is quicker and also produces a roast with a crackly surface of fat and a maximum of drippings. The second method requires no chaperoning, it goes on its own merry way, but the outside fat will not be so crisp nor will the drippings be as rich as those resulting from the first method. Try both ways and decide for yourself which one you prefer.

One pound of meat (with the bone in) will yield approximately two servings. Be sure you make a note of the exact weight of the roast you have purchased. If you have a meat thermometer, this isn't too important, but if you have not, then it is essential that you know exactly how much the meat weighs.

Take the meat from its wrapping and store it in the refrigerator loosely wrapped in waxed paper until ½ hour or so before you want to start roasting it. Then wipe the meat well with a cloth wrung out in cold water. Pat it dry and with a sharp knife trim off the hard edges of the fat. If there seems to be too much fat on the meat, trim some of that away too. But remember that the fat acts as an automatic "baster" so be sure to leave enough, otherwise the roast will be dry and tough.

Allow your roast to "chambré" (that is, to come to room temperature) for at least ½ hour before you put it in a preheated oven.

It doesn't make a terrific amount of difference whether you season your meat before or after it is cooked. One school of thought claims that to salt the meat before cooking will toughen it; on the other hand, salting does emphasize the flavor. If you wish to sprinkle meat with salt, use about 1 teaspoon of salt to 1 pound of meat.

Also optional is the use of flour. A little flour rubbed lightly into the meat will add to the color of the gravy. Do, by all means, use your meat thermometer. Be sure that the bulb of the thermometer is in the exact center of the meat and does not touch either fat or bone. Measure your thermometer against the cut side of the meat and you will be able to judge quite accurately how far to insert it.

A one-rib roast should be put flat side down on the trivet— or rack—in the bottom of the roasting pan; for roasts involving more than one rib you need not use the rack, simply put the prepared roast in the pan, with the fat side of the roast facing up.

DO NOT COVER THE ROAST. Meat cooked with the top on the roasting pan is not roasted, it is braised, which is quite a different thing.

DO NOT ADD WATER. This will steam the meat, not roast it.

DO NOT BASTE. If you place the fat side of the meat up, it will baste itself.

DO NOT TURN THE ROAST.

BE SURE YOU KNOW HOW MUCH THE ROAST WEIGHS. Don't trust your memory; write the weight on the outside of the package when you buy the meat and either keep the wrapping or make a notation before you discard the wrapping.

QUICK-COOKING METHOD

For a standing rib roast, approximately 5½–8 pounds.

Oven Temperature	Minutes per Pound	Thermometer Reading
Rare		
500 degrees for the first 15 minutes 350 degrees thereafter	19 minutes	140
Medium		
500 degrees for the first 15 minutes 350 degrees thereafter	24 minutes	160
Well done		
500 degrees for the first 15 minutes 350 degrees thereafter	29 minutes	170

For a roast weighing between 3 and 5½ pounds, add a slightly longer cooking time—about 2–3 minutes to the pound.

For a rolled roast, allow 5–10 minutes longer roasting time to the pound.

ONE-TEMPERATURE METHOD

For a standing rib roast, approximately 5½–8 pounds.

Oven Temperature	Minutes per Pound	Thermometer Reading
Rare		
325 degrees	21	140
Medium		
325 degrees	27	160
Well Done		
325 degrees	33	170

For rolled roasts and smaller cuts, follow the times given under the QUICK-COOKING METHOD.

It is a good idea to calculate the cooking time in advance and to make a note of the approximate time that the roast should be done.

Here are two ways of cooking spareribs. One of the many attractions of spareribs is that they require almost no attention whatsoever. These recipes will serve four to six people.

Barbecued Spareribs

With a damp cloth, wipe off about 4 pounds of spareribs and cut down in between the ribs so that you have serving-sized pieces. Arrange them in a shallow roasting pan with the meatier side up.

Slice 1 lemon and 1 onion, and put a slice of each on top of the spareribs. Have your oven preheated to 450° and roast the spareribs for 30 minutes.

Combine the following ingredients in a saucepan: 1 cup catsup, ⅓ cup Worcestershire sauce, 1 teaspoon salt, a little Tabasco, and 1¾ cups water.

Mix 1 tablespoon chili powder with ¼ cup water and add that too.

Place the saucepan over a medium to high flame and bring the sauce to a boil.

Pour the sauce over the ribs when they have roasted ½ hour and continue roasting them for 45 minutes more, basting them every 15 minutes. To baste means to spoon or pour liquid over whatever you may be cooking, usually roasting. Use a baster if you have one; this is a long glass or metal tube with a rubber bulb at one end. To pull the juice into the tube, squeeze the bulb and release; squeeze the bulb again to spray the juice or sauce over the meat. This device is a great aid in preventing burned wrists and forearms. If the sauce seems to reduce too much, that is, cook away, add a little more water.

Spareribs with Sweet and Sour Sauce

For four people you will want 4 pounds of spareribs.

Proceed as for barbecued spareribs except that the lemon and onion are omitted; instead, with a small brush, slather ribs generously on either side with soy sauce.

Place them in a shallow roasting pan in a 350° oven for about 1¼–1½ hours.

Halfway through the roasting time, get out your kitchen tongs and turn ribs over.

About ½ hour before the ribs are done, start making the following sauce:

First, prepare and put to one side 1 tablespoon chopped, preserved ginger or 2 teaspoons scraped fresh ginger root, ½ cup pineapple chunks or slices of pineapple cut into little wedges, and ½ cup already-sliced sweet pickles, roughly chopped.

Into a saucepan measure 1 cup sugar, ½ cup Madeira wine, 2 tablespoons soy sauce.

To this add 1 green pepper which has been cleaned and cut into narrow strips. (Classic Chinese recipes always direct that the peppers be cut into 8 sections.)

Place the saucepan on a medium to high flame and bring to a boil.

Mix 1 tablespoon cornstarch with enough water to make a thin paste, and add this to the boiling sauce; turn the flame down a little.

Cook until the sauce is thick and glossy. You must stir it constantly after the cornstarch has been added.

Just before serving, stir in the ginger, pineapple, and pickles. When the ribs are done, remove them to a hot platter, pour the sauce over them, and serve with boiled rice.

Croque-Monsieur

This is a very expansible recipe. If you make these sandwiches in small sizes, they are excellent with cocktails; in large sizes—

with or without a béchamel sauce—they make a substantial enough dinner or luncheon dish.

Butter 2 slices of white bread per person and sprinkle half of the slices with grated Parmesan or Gruyère cheese.

Cover the cheese with a thin slice of boiled or baked ham and sprinkle the ham with additional cheese and some freshly ground pepper.

Cover each ham-and-bread combination with the remaining slice of bread and remove the crusts. If you want the sandwiches for cocktails, cut them into fingers or halves or little squares.

For 8 slices of bread, melt 3 tablespoons butter in a shallow pan and brush the sandwiches with a generous amount of the melted butter.

Put the sandwiches on a cookie sheet or baking pan. If you aren't going to use them immediately, they will keep in the refrigerator, covered with waxed paper.

Preheat the oven to 450° and bake the sandwiches until they are an attractive golden brown.

If you want to use them as an entree, the procedure is somewhat different.

Have the ham about ¼ inch thick and some Swiss cheese of the same thickness. Make as many sandwiches as you need of white bread, a slice of ham, and a slice of cheese, topped off with a slice of bread. Cut the crusts off with a sharp knife, and cut the sandwiches in half. If they won't stick together, tie them together with a little kitchen thread or string (to be removed before serving).

Make the **Béchamel Sauce** (p. 56).

Shortly before serving, sauté the sandwiches in a large frying pan in which you have heated some butter and a little cooking oil until very hot. Turn the sandwiches once. They are done when they are golden on both sides.

Arrange them on a serving dish and pour the sauce in the center.

Rolled Sandwiches
If you want to use pumpernickel bread for rolled sandwiches, have the loaf sliced very thin. To prevent the slices from breaking, roll each one with a rolling pin before adding the filling.

Veal and Spinach

With a sharp knife, trim 3 or 4 veal chops neatly. Sprinkle both sides of each chop with a mixture of salt and pepper and let the chops stand.

Melt 1 tablespoon butter in a saucepan, and when it is foamy put in the veal trimmings, 1 slice uncooked bacon, 1 peeled and sliced onion, 1 carrot cut into small pieces, and a bouquet composed of a few sprigs of parsley, 1 bay leaf, and a sprig of thyme. Let this cook until it begins to brown, and then sprinkle with a little flour—perhaps 5 tablespoons—and stir and cook for 2–3 minutes more.

Then add 3 tablespoons sherry, 1 tablespoon tomato paste, and 1 tablespoon milk. Season and bring to a boil, and then reduce the heat and allow to simmer for 15 minutes. Stir from time to time.

Cook and drain a box of frozen, chopped spinach, and mix with a little cream and butter.

Fry the veal chops in about 3 tablespoons butter—more, depending upon the size of the chops.

Spread the spinach on a serving dish, place the chops on top of the spinach, and pour the sauce (from which the bouquet has been removed) through a strainer over the meat.

Omelette Paysanne

For two or three people, use 4–6 eggs, depending on the state of your appetite.

Fry 3 slices bacon until crisp and crumble them into small bits. Or you may cut the bacon into little squares with the aid of your kitchen scissors and then fry them. Drain the bacon.

In the fat remaining in the skillet, fry 1 medium-sized boiled diced potato. Drain the potato cubes and sprinkle them very lightly with salt. Potatoes absorb a lot of fat whilst frying; don't be afraid to add extra bacon drippings, butter, or margarine. If you really want to go all out on this, you may also prepare ½ onion, finely chopped, and ½ green pepper, treated likewise. All the vegetables and the bacon may be fried together over a medium flame, or the bacon and potatoes may be fried together if you aren't going to use the onion and pepper.

Break the eggs into a bowl, add a pinch of salt and pepper, and beat lightly with a fork.

Add the vegetables and bacon. A fairly thick iron pan may be used; if you are a French cook, your omelette pan will be used for omelettes and nothing else. See that the pan is perfectly clean, rub it with a little salt and a paper towel to be sure there are no places where the omelette may stick. The pan or skillet should be very, very hot—smoking, in fact.

Put a small piece of butter in the pan and swirl it around, add the eggs quickly, and shake the pan and stir the eggs. With the flat of your fork lift the eggs and tip the pan slightly to let the uncooked parts of the eggs run to the edge. Run the fork around the sides of the pan. Tip the pan away from you and again run the flat of the fork under the part of the omelette nearest you; turn this half over on the opposite half of the omelette and roll the whole thing out onto a serving dish.

A properly cooked French omelette takes only a few seconds to cook—remember the pan must be smoking-hot—you don't have to use butter in your pan either, bacon fat is fine and you run less risk of your omelette sticking if you use it. Another thing to remember is that an overcooked egg is a tough egg.

A Spanish omelette always has the potatoes, onion, and pepper in it and a peeled and deseeded, finely cut-up tomato as well. This omelette is not turned in half, but cooked on both sides and a little longer than the French variety, then turned like a pancake and served flat. In Spain it is eaten hot or cold; it is (or was in my day) always included in every box lunch put up for travelers.

Eggs in Mustard Sauce

Soft-cook 4 eggs for about 3 minutes.

Shell them very, very carefully under hot water and put them on a cloth to drain.

Chop or snip enough parsley to make 1 tablespoon, and cut 6 tablespoons butter into small pieces.

Put the butter and parsley in a saucepan together with ¼ cup prepared mustard, 1 tablespoon wine vinegar, and salt and pepper. Heat this slightly and then add the eggs, which you have cut in halves. Take care when you cut the eggs as the insides should be runny—better have a small plate or bowl handy.

Cook the eggs and sauce together, shaking the pan continuously to combine the yolks and butter to make the sauce smooth and creamy.

Serve spooned over halves of toasted, buttered English muffins or slices of toast.

Oysters and Ham

Drain the liquor from ½ pint loose (shelled, that is) oysters. You may buy oysters already shucked in a cardboard carton. Put the oysters in a colander or sieve and run water over to wash them and to remove any remaining bits of shell.

Trim the excess fat from 2 slices of ham, cut about ⅛ inch thick.

Put about 1 teaspoon butter in a skillet over a medium-high flame and cook the slices of ham very lightly. Don't brown them.

Transfer the ham to a hot serving dish and pour 6 tablespoons cream into the pan in which you cooked the ham. Turn up the flame a bit and bring the cream to a boil.

Season the hot cream with a little salt, pepper, and a drop of Tabasco and Worcestershire sauce.

Add a teaspoon of butter and stir.

Put in the oysters and cook until the edges begin to ruffle or curl. This takes only about 3–5 minutes.

Pour the cream and oysters over the hot ham and serve and eat immediately.

If ½ pint of oysters seems too little, you may use 1 pint of oysters and increase the cream to ½ cup.

Chicken and Ham

Wipe off the pieces of chicken and wrap each piece in a thin slice of ham—preferably the smoked variety. Secure the ham with a string or kitchen thread and stick 3 or 4 whole cloves into the ham slices.

Grease or butter a shallow baking pan and put the chicken in it, breast side up.

Mix together 2 tablespoons brown sugar, 1 tablespoon flour, and a dash of pepper. Smear this over the ham.

Bake in a preheated, moderately hot (400°) oven until the fat starts to run. Reduce the heat to 350° and add a little stock or water, enough to cover the bottom of the pan to a depth of about ¼ inch.

Grate, or mince very fine, 1 small onion, and sprinkle this in the baking pan together with 1 (or even 2) tablespoons of butter cut into little pieces.

Bake about 35 minutes, or until the chicken is done.

Ham and Kidney Bean Casserole

Trim the fat from 1 pound tenderized ham, about ½ inch thick, cut up roughly, and put to one side.

Cut the ham into small cubes.

Melt 2 tablespoons butter in a fair-sized casserole, add the ham fat and 1 finely chopped clove garlic, cook until lightly browned over medium heat.

161

Stir in ¼ teaspoon salt and 2 teaspoons (or more, if you like it) of curry powder.

When these ingredients are combined (well mixed, that is), add 1 can kidney beans with the liquid from the can, a generous cup of sliced onions, 1 *small* "head" celery—the whole white stalk—cut into ½ inch pieces, and 1 good tablespoon minced parsley. Mix all together well, put the lid on the casserole, and bake in a preheated (for 10 minutes beforehand) 400° oven for 45 minutes.

Remove the cover and bake for 15–20 minutes more. Don't allow the liquid to dry out. Serve in hot soup bowls or individual casseroles.

These are the amounts of ingredients for the bigger casserole: 3 cans kidney beans, 2½ pounds (in 2 slices) tenderized ham, 4 cups sliced onions, 2 small heads celery, 4 tablespoons butter, 2 teaspoons or more curry powder, 3 tablespoons minced parsley, ½ teaspoon salt, and 2 cloves garlic. The procedure is exactly the same.

Stuffed Green Peppers or Tomatoes

Stuffed green peppers or tomatoes are a fine way to utilize leftovers. Leftover stuffing or frozen stuffing could be used up this way.

For green peppers—wash the peppers, cut off the stem ends, and cut the peppers in half lengthwise. Remove the veins and seeds.

Rub the peppers all over the exterior with margarine, oil, or bacon drippings.

Spoon whatever leftovers you may wish to use into the cavities. Don't pack the stuffing into the peppers too tightly or they will burst at the seams.

Place them in a baking pan with a little water in the bottom of it and bake in a moderate (350°) oven until they are tender.

See directions on page 121 for hollowing out tomatoes. After the tomatoes have drained about 15 minutes, fill them with any cooked leftovers you may have on hand. The stuffing should be slightly moistened, using a little canned bouillon, cream, or gravy. If the tomatoes are somewhat inclined to spread, ease them into greased muffin tins. Be sure to pour a little water into any empty compartments of the muffin tins so that the pan will not burn.

Ham and Cheese Pie

Buy about 1 pound of ham in a 1-inch slice. Trim off most of the fat and make a few slashes around the edge so that the ham won't curl up when it's cooked.

Melt a little of the fat in a frying pan and sauté the meat. Sauté means to fry lightly.

Peel, core, and slice 2 apples into rings.

Put the ham in a deep ovenproof dish and dispose the apple rings over it.

Mix together ½ cup dark brown sugar, 2 tablespoons butter, and ½ cup flour, and crumble this with your fingers over the apples.

Buy the already-sliced packaged American cheese (processed) and arrange the slices over the ham-apple-crumb combination.

Pour 1 cup sour cream over the whole business. Bake in a 350° oven for 1 hour, basting several times. Use that long baster and save the burned arm. If it seems to dry out, add a little water.

Leftovers with Noodles

Cook 1 cup noodles in 1 quart boiling water to which ¼ teaspoon salt has been added. This amount will yield 2 cups cooked noodles.

163

Add 2 teaspoons oil or margarine to the boiling water and then drop in the noodles. Cook them for about 20 minutes, dump them into a colander, rinse, and drain.

Grease a shallow ovenproof glass dish or a deep pie plate and arrange a layer of noodles on the bottom. Sprinkle the noodles with whatever leftovers in the way of meat or vegetables you may have around. You should have about ½ cup meat, ground or diced, and combined with 2 tablespoons each of chopped green pepper and celery. Put another layer of noodles over the meat, and so on until you have used all your ingredients.

Make a custard by lightly beating 1 whole egg into 1 cup milk seasoned with ¼ teaspoon salt and a dash of pepper. Pour the custard over the noodles-and-meat arrangement.

Cover with a thick layer of bread crumbs and bake in a 350° oven for about 45 minutes. Check to see if the custard is cooked by poking a toothpick in it. If it does not come out clean, cook an additional 10–15 minutes.

SALADS

Cold Soup Salad

Hard-cook 2 or 3 eggs, that is, place the eggs in their shells in a small saucepan, cover with cold water, bring to a boil (i.e., when the water bubbles energetically), lower the heat, and simmer (when the bubbles just break the surface of the water occasionally) for 15 minutes.

Remove the pan from the fire and run cold water over the eggs. This will help prevent an unattractive dark ring around the egg yolk and also make peeling easier.

Now, chop 1 small- to medium-sized onion very fine, take 1 small cucumber—you may either peel it or wash it off and chop it fine, ditto 1 green pepper. Before you chop the green pepper, wash it, cut off the stem end and, with a small, sharp knife, remove the seeds; also cut out the whitish "ribs" or veins inside.

Crush 1 clove (toe) of garlic—peeled, of course. To do this, sprinkle the garlic with a little salt and mash it with either the dull edge or the flat of your cleaver. The object of the salt is to discourage the garlic from sticking to the knife, garlic being a very "greasy" bulb.

Slice 1 lemon or 1 lime as thin as you can—wash it first—and squeeze another lemon or 2 limes. If you lean on the lemon or limes and roll them under the palm of your hand before you

165

squeeze them, you'll extract all the juice. Strain the juice through a little strainer.

Dice a couple of slices of stale bread and fry the cubes in a small pan with a little cooking oil until they are golden. Remove them to a piece of paper toweling or brown paper to drain. This drains the surplus grease and leaves the "croutons" crisp. You also do the same thing with bacon or anything you have fried and want in a degreased condition.

Peel the cooled, hard-cooked eggs; carefully run a knife around and through the whites and take out the yolks. Put them in a good-sized bowl and add 2 tablespoons olive oil to them. With a wooden spoon, mash the yolks and the oil together and work them to a smooth paste, working against the side of the bowl.

Add the garlic, 1½ teaspoons Worcestershire sauce, 1 teaspoon *dry* mustard, a dash of Tabasco sauce, salt and pepper to taste, and 1 quart tomato juice. Mix well and add the chopped-up onion, cucumber, and green pepper.

Stir some more and put the soup in the refrigerator to chill for at least 3 hours; about 1–1½ hours in a freezer.

Before you serve the soup, cut the remaining egg whites and some pimiento into narrow strips; add to the soup. Add also one or two ice cubes, if desired, and sprinkle the croutons on the top. Be sure your soup bowls are cold.

Avocado and Caviar

Try to choose a ripe avocado or alligator pear. Cut the pear in half lengthwise and remove the large seed. Remove any of the papery covering from the seed that may cling to the cavity.

Squeeze a little lemon juice on the insides of the halves to prevent them from discoloring.

Put a tablespoon of red caviar in the center of each half and chill well. Serve as a first course.

166

Corn Salad

Drain the contents of one No. 2 (large) can of whole kernel corn, add to it 1 drained, chopped pimiento, 1 chopped small onion, 1 chopped green pepper (remember to remove seeds and ribs).

Mix the whole thing with some French dressing and serve on a leaf of lettuce. This should be chilled too.

Ham and Swiss Cheese Salad

Dice 1 cup—½ pound—precooked ham. Or you could substitute any tinned meat you happen to like. Also dice 1 cup Swiss cheese, not the processed kind, but the real Swiss cheese, preferably, which has holes in it. Dice 1 small onion and ½ cup celery. Mix all this together, adding any cold leftover vegetable or a small can green peas, with a little mayonnaise thinned out with lemon juice. Garnish the salad with sliced or quartered hard-cooked eggs.

Mix-Up Salad

This is a wonderful "clean-out-the-refrigerator" salad. I hope you have lots of leftovers on hand, because you will need a few tablespoons each of the following (a little bit one way or the other makes no difference—anything goes!):

About 3–4 tablespoons cold, boiled potatoes cut into cubes, an equal amount of cold, cooked carrots and string beans.

Mix all this together and pour over enough French dressing to coat the ingredients well, about ⅛ cup.

Let this marinate (or soak) in the refrigerator at least an hour.

Just before serving, mix in 1 tablespoon chopped sweet pickle, 1 hard-cooked egg, also chopped, and ¼–⅓ cup mayonnaise. Toss.

167

Chili, Aspic, and Avocado Salad

Pour half the contents of a large bottle of chili sauce into a saucepan and add to it ¼ green pepper, cleaned and minced, and 1 chopped green onion (top and roots removed), a little Tabasco, ½ teaspoon salt, and ½ cup water.

Let this combination simmer over low heat for 12–15 minutes, stirring from time to time.

Soak 1 tablespoon gelatin in ¼ cup cold water for 5 minutes, and then add this to the hot chili sauce. Beat the mixture until it has cooled somewhat. You may hasten this process by putting the saucepan in a bowl of cold water.

When cooled, pour the mixture into a shallow, greased glass dish, mold, or a refrigerator tray, and put it in the refrigerator or freezer to set. You don't really have to go to all the fuss of a mold, although it looks very pretty; you can just scoop out the aspic with a tablespoon and put it on a lettuce leaf, surround it with segments of peeled avocado or alligator pear, and serve.

Poppy Seed Dressing

Combine ¾ cup sugar; 2 teaspoons dry mustard; 2 teaspoons salt; ⅜ cup wine vinegar; ⅜ cup lemon juice; 3 tablespoons onion juice or 1½ heaping teaspoons of granulated onion. Add 2 cups oil (not olive) slowly, beating well until thickened. Add 3 tablespoons poppy seed; stir and store. Yield: one pint.

SALAD DRESSINGS

Curry Salad Dressing

The following dressing is nice on a salad of hard-cooked eggs:

Thin out ½ cup mayonnaise with vinegar and add to it ½ teaspoon curry powder, or more, according to your taste. Mix well.

Or:

Mix together ½ teaspoon curry powder with ¾ teaspoon salt, and add 1 tablespoon French dressing and mix well. When thoroughly combined, add ½ cup more French dressing.

French Dressing with Olives

Add 4 tablespoons chopped, ripe olives to ½ cup French dressing. If the olives are the already chopped, canned kind, be sure to drain them first. Grate ½ teaspoon onion and chop the same amount of parsley. Add these ingredients to the dressing and mix well. Serve over a green salad.

Russian Dressing (really Thousand Island dressing)

Thin 1 cup mayonnaise with ¼ cup light cream and add to it 2 tablespoons chili sauce. Mince the following and add to the mayonnaise: 2 tablespoons stuffed olives, 1 tablespoon green pepper, and 1 tablespoon minced onion.

169

DESSERTS

Here are four quite dress-up desserts, but very easy ones. You may do them on the stove or, if you have a chafing dish, they may be done at the table, which adds a nice fillip.

Whiskey Apples

Peel the rind thin from ½ lemon and then squeeze and strain the juice from the remaining half.

Put 6 tablespoons sugar in a pan, or in the top pan of a chafing dish over a low flame, and combine with the lemon juice a 1-inch piece of cinnamon stick and 4 ounces bourbon. Bring this to a boil.

Have ready 4 eating apples, peeled and cored, and put them in the boiling sauce. Place the top on the pan and let the apples simmer about 35 minutes, or until tender. Spoon the sauce over the apples before you serve them.

Flaming Peaches

There are 2 ways of making this dessert—with either fresh or canned peaches. First, with canned peaches:

Pour the liquid from a 1 pint can or jar of peach halves into a shallow pan. Place on a medium flame and bring to a boil.

Dissolve ½ teaspoon arrowroot or cornstarch in a little cold water, just enough to make a thin paste.

Place the peaches in the hot juice and put a little of the arrowroot mixture on each half peach. Baste the peaches until they are heated.

Pour 2 ounces or 4 tablespoons of brandy or bourbon over the peaches and set aflame.

Fresh peaches:

Bring a little water to a boil in a small saucepan and into it drop 1 fresh peach for each person to be served. Let the peaches poach for 2 or 3 minutes in order to facilitate peeling. Remove the fruit from the saucepan, drain, and peel.

Put the whole peaches in a chafing dish or shallow copper pan over a medium flame, pour in some kirsch—enough to generously cover the bottom of the pan; with a fork prick the peaches in a few places.

When the kirsch becomes hot, it will flame up; shake the pan while the liqueur is burning and sprinkle the peaches with a little powdered sugar.

Serve immediately.

Cherries Jubilee

If you can get the black Bing cherries already pitted, do so; otherwise, you may use the unpitted variety. You need, for four people, a pint jar of cherries.

Pour the juice into a pan and bring to a boil.

In a small cup dissolve ½ teaspoon arrowroot or cornstarch in a little cold water and stir until it makes a paste.

Add the cherries to the hot juice and then add the arrowroot mixture. Stir until well heated; pour in 4 tablespoons kirsch and set alight.

Or you may pour ¼ cup brandy over the cherries, light and,

171

after the flame has died down, mix in 2 tablespoons kirsch. This may be served alone or poured over vanilla ice cream.

Fresh Strawberries in Wine

Strawberries are good with a little sugar sprinkled over them and mixed with about ¼ cup red wine and then chilled. A little lemon juice strained over sugared, prepared strawberries, the whole then chilled, is nice too.

Sauce for a Fruit Compote

Melt ½ cup currant jelly over a low flame.

When it is entirely melted, add 2 tablespoons kirsch—more if you like—and mix this with whatever fruits you are using, then chill.

Strawberries, peaches, cherries, and pineapple all combine well to make a fruit compote. Don't use the above sauce for a mixture of fruits containing melon of any kind.

Mélange of Fruit

Mix diced, fresh pineapple with sections of grapefruit and oranges. Sprinkle the compote liberally with orange juice and strawberry juice. Serve cold.

Chocolate Pears

Chill a jar of brandied pears and serve them for dessert with chocolate sauce poured over them.

Strawberry Tart

Bake a pie shell, that is, the bottom crust only. Be sure to prick the bottom and sides of the pastry well before baking so that the crust won't shrink. The amounts I am giving will fill a 9-inch pie shell. Cool the shell.

Wash and remove the stems from 2 pint boxes of fresh strawberries. Drain them in a colander and from them choose the prettiest berries and put them aside. You will need about half of the amount of berries that you have. Mash the remaining half of the fruit through a sieve or in an electric blender. If you use a blender, strain the juice.

Pour the juice into a saucepan and add 1 cup sugar into which you have already mixed 3 tablespoons cornstarch. Place the saucepan over a medium-high flame and stir constantly until the mixture is thick and transparent. Cool.

Mash one small (3-ounce) package cream cheese and beat well with enough cream to make it fluffy. Spread this mixture on the bottom of the baked pie shell.

Arrange your berries on top of the cheese and pour the cooled juice over them. Chill.

Cornstarch as a thickening agent is frowned upon by our better chefs, but if you have no arrowroot handy—and I don't know many who have—use cornstarch instead.

Mocha Mousse

Cream ⅓ cup butter—that means to work the butter with the back of a spoon against the side of a bowl until it reaches a light and fluffy or creamy consistency. It's much simpler to use an electric beater, if you have one.

Add ¾ cup brown sugar very gradually, mixing it into the butter, and then ¾ cup strong, black coffee very, very slowly— just a few drops at a time.

Add ½ teaspoon vanilla extract.

Dip 2 dozen lady fingers in coffee and make a layer of some of them in the bottom of a refrigerator tray lined with waxed paper, or a deep glass "bread tin."

Spoon a layer of the mocha cream on top of the lady fingers, and then put another layer of lady fingers on top of that. Continue this process until you have used all the lady fingers and mocha cream. It's best to finish with a layer of lady fingers, if possible.

Cover with waxed paper and put a weight on top. That's why I like the "bread tin" type of mold, because I use a brick for the weight and it just fits. This should be in a refrigerator overnight or in a freezer about 4 hours.

Plantation Pecan Cake

Chop very very fine enough shelled pecans to fill 3 cups. Sift 3 tablespoons cake flour, sprinkle with 1 teaspoon baking powder, and sift twice more. Mix with the chopped nuts. Separate 6 eggs. Beat the whites (sprinkle with a pinch of salt) until they stand up in peaks when the beater is withdrawn. Heap the egg whites on the nut-flour mixture and gently fold them in, turning the mixture over and over. DO NOT STIR OR BEAT.

Preheat your oven to 375 degrees.

Sift 1½ cups granulated sugar.

Beat the 6 egg yolks very well, until they are light and lemon-colored. Stir in the sugar and beat well again.

Lightly oil and flour two cake pans, filling them with batter, about two thirds full.

Place the pans in the preheated oven, allowing enough room between them so that there will be a circulation of air.

After 20 minutes test the cake with a wire cake tester, straw, or toothpick; whichever instrument you use should be perfectly clean when withdrawn from the cake, although perhaps one or two crumbs are allowable. The cake should also be slightly browned on top and have begun to shrink from the sides of the pan. Another test is to press the top of the cake with your finger; if it is done, the cake will spring back into shape and no indentation will remain.

Remove the pans from the oven and turn them upside down until they are completely cooled. Remove layers by running a knife around the edges and beneath them. If the edges are hard, scape them with a sharp knife.

You may spread the bottom layer with sweetened whipped cream, place the second layer on top of it and sprinkle lightly with confectioners' sugar, or, if you prefer, the following filling: Pour ½ cup corn syrup into a saucepan and cook to a light thread. The syrup should be thick enough to form a thread between thumb and finger. Pour slowly over 2 well-beaten egg whites, beating slowly all the time. Continue beating until thick. Spread between the layers of the cake.

Saucey Tip

Thin honey with a little Sauterne wine to make a thin sauce for French toast. Use Sauterne for part of liquid when making lemon sauce.

Cooking Guide

Kitchen arithmetic: Count on using at least half a cup of medium white sauce to a cup of cooked diced vegetables or chicken for a creamed dish.

Use ordinary
ice cream recipe
for measuring
1 cup of butter
vanilla etc.

HEAT canned cling peach halves in broiler or oven. Fill centers with dairy sour cream seasoned with prepared horseradish. Use as garnish for meat loaf, beef roast, burger patties.

STUFFED TOMATOES MANHATTAN

Cut a slice from the stem end of each of 6 tomatoes, cutting edges petal fashion if desired. Scoop out tomato pulp. Drain tomatoes thoroughly. Chill. Combine 1 cup dairy sour cream with ½ envelope onion soup mix. Add one avocado, peeled and diced, and ¼ teaspoon hot pepper sauce. Chill several hours. To serve, spoon chilled mixture into tomato cups. Yield: 6 portions.

STUFFED TOMATOES ANTIPASTO

Cut a slice from the stem end of each of 6 tomatoes, cutting edges petal fashion if desired. Scoop out tomato pulp. Drain tomatoes thoroughly. Chill. Combine 2 cans (6½ or 7 ounces each) tuna in vegetable oil, 6 radishes, chopped, and ¼ cup ripe olives, chopped. Add ½ cup Italian garlic dressing and 1 garlic clove. Chill 1 hour or longer. Remove garlic. Spoon chilled mixture into tomato cups. Yield: 6 portions. (THE END)

THE HAPPY, HAPPY ENDING

As a glorious finale to a gala dinner or buffet party there is nothing more festive than **Iced Coffee Diabolique.** It is not only delectable, but also guaranteed to keep your party going until all hours.

I feel that French drip coffee is the best to use for this delightful concoction, but if you must use another variety, then be sure you make it strong, strong, strong. It should be, as the French saying goes, "black as the Devil, hot as hell, and strong as love!"

To serve eight people, make 4 cups of coffee. Pour the hot coffee into a generous-sized pitcher and add the peel of ½ orange, 2 sticks cinnamon, 12 whole cloves, and 3 tablespoonfuls sugar —more if you like. Stir this a bit and then pour in 1 cup brandy and stir some more. Cool. Taste it, add more brandy if it seems indicated; some types of coffee seem to "absorb" more brandy than others.

When you are ready to serve, half-fill slender glasses with crushed ice, pour in the coffee through a strainer so that the spices and peel remain in the pitcher.

A parfait glass is perfect for this coffee, or a small Pilsener-type of glass.

Iced Coffee Diabolique, together with crisp cookies, lady fingers, or macaroons, makes a complete dessert at any time of the year.

Index

Chicken Hash with Noodles, 91-92

Chicken heart, 90

Chicken Livers
leftover, 98
in Red Wine, 99, 102-3

Chicken soup, 91, 92-93; in Petites Marmites, 99

Chicory, 34

Chili, Aspic, and Avocado Salad, 168

Chili, Quick, 113-14

Chili powder, 114

Chipped Beef and Cream Cheese, 65-66

Chocolate
measurements, 23
melting, 15

Chocolate Cookies, 140

Chocolate Pears, 172

Chopping, defined, 75

Chopping board, 24

Chutney, defined, 83

Chutney Canapés, 81, 83

Cider vinegar, 39-40

Citrus fruits, 34, 35
to freeze, 50
knife for, 18
See also Lemons and Oranges

Clam and Tomato Bouillon, 131, 132

Clams, 31

Clam Stew, 149

Cleaver, 24, 175

Cocktails, food for, 64-66; see also Canapés and Hors d'Oeuvres

Cocktail spreads

Cream Cheese and Chipped beef, 65-66

Cream Cheese and Onions, 65

Roquefort Cheese and Red Caviar, 66

Sour Cream and Red Caviar, 64

Coeur à la Crème, 116, 117

Coffee, 36
Diabolique, Iced, 176
Drip, 63
Drip, New Orleans, 62-63
Percolated, 63

Colander, 24

Cole Slaw, 113, 114

Compote, Fruit, 172

Confectioners' sugar, 39

Cookies, Chocolate, 140

Cookie sheet, 24

Cooking oil, 20, 75

Cooking terms, defined, 19-21; see also individual terms

Copper, to clean, 48

Corn, 33; canned, 36

Corn Bread, 113, 115

Corn Salad, 167

Corn syrup, 39

Crab "boil," 18

Crab Meat Mongol, 150-51

Crab Meat Piquante, 116-17

Crabs, 31

Cream, 36
to sour, 16
whipping, measurements, 23

Cream, to, defined, 173

Cream Cheese and Chipped Beef, 65-66

181

String Bean and Potato Salad, 94
String beans, 32
  with Almonds, 133, 134
  "Frenched," 39
  frozen, 39, 88, 90
  leftover, 94, 162, 167
Succotash, frozen, 136, 137
Suet, defined, 113
Sugar
  kinds of, 39
  measurements, 23
  substitutes for, 39
"Sunshine" cake, 86
Sweetbreads, 30
Sweet and Sour Sauce, 156
Swiss chard, 33
Swiss Cheese Salad, Ham and, 167
Syrups, kinds of, 38-39

Tables, miscellaneous, 22-23
Tangerines, 35
Tart, Brown Betty, 133-34
Tart, Strawberry, 172-73
Tartare Sauce, 57
Tarte Lorraine, 131
Temperatures, oven, 22
Terms, cooking, defined, 19-21;
  see also individual terms
Thickening agents, 173
Thousand Island Dressing, 169
Toast, defined, 21
Tomato Bouillon, Clam and, 131,
  132
Tomatoes
  to hollow out, 121
  measurements, 23
  to peel, 15, 96-97

Stuffed, 162, 163
  Stuffed with Rice, Cold, 121
Tomato Indienne, 120, 121
Tongue, 30
Towels, to wash, 48-49
Tripe, 30
Trout, Baked Fillet of, 76
Turkey, 32

Utility knife, 24

Variety meats, 29-30
Veal
  amounts to buy for two, 43
  cuts of, 30
  leftover, 108, 111
  Roast, 30, 108-9, 111
  Cold, 111
Veal Chops
  Baked in Sour Cream, 138
  in Jelly, 81-82
  and Spinach, 158
Veal hearts, 30
Vegetable fat, 19
Vegetables, 32-34
  amounts to buy for two, 42
  brush for, 25
  to freeze, 50
  to keep hot, 16
  leafy, 33, 34
  marinated (Russian Salad), 91
  Raw, as hors d'oeuvres, 65
Velouté Sauce, 56
Viennese Cream, Frozen, 96
Vinaigrette Sauce, 74-75
Vinegar, kinds of, 39-40

191

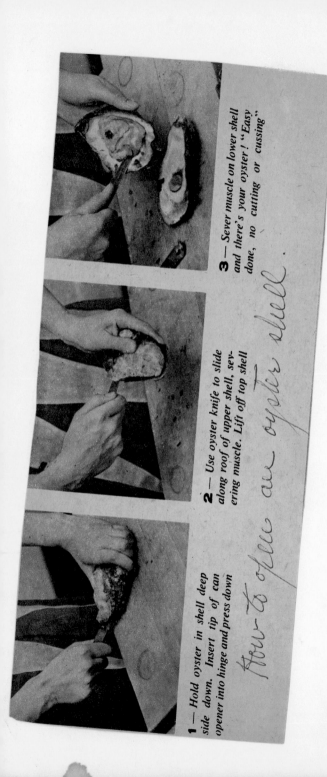

1 — Hold oyster in shell deep side down. Insert tip of can opener into hinge and press down

2 — Use oyster knife to slide along roof of upper shell, severing muscle. Lift off top shell

3 — Sever muscle on lower shell and there's your oyster! "Easy done, no cutting or cussing"

How to open an oyster shell.

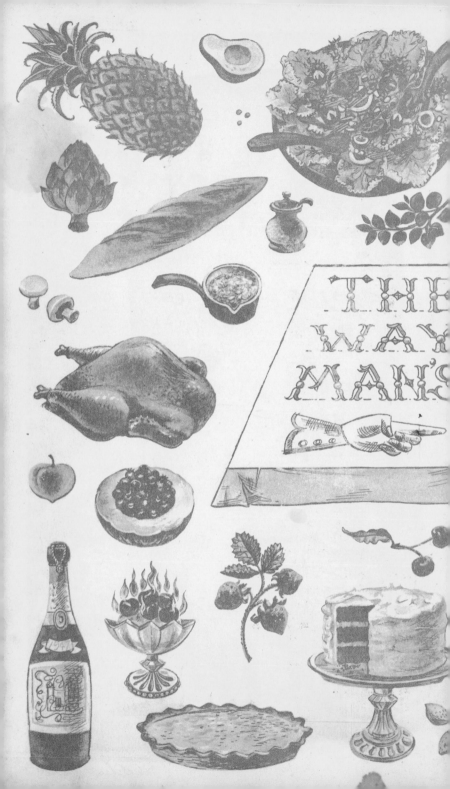